Burning Bush
and Broken Bread

Burning Bush and Broken Bread

Implications of a Communicating God

Richard Berryman

Anglican Book Centre
Toronto, Canada

Morehouse-Barlow
Wilton, Connecticut

1987
Anglican Book Centre
600 Jarvis Street
Toronto, Ontario
Canada M4Y 2J6

Morehouse-Barlow
78 Danbury Road
Wilton, Connecticut
USA 06897

Typesetting by Jay Tee Graphics Ltd.
Printed in Canada.

Canadian Cataloguing in Publication Data

Berryman, Richard
  Burning bush and broken bread

ISBN 0-919891-66-7

1. Communication (Theology). 2. Witness bearing
(Christianity). 3. Story-telling (Christian
theology). 4. Christian art and symbolism.
I. Title.

BV4319.B47 1987   248.4   C87-093783-9

Library of Congress Cataloging-in-Publication Data

Berryman, Richard.
  Burning bush and broken bread.

  Bibliography: p.
  1. Meditations. I. Title.
BV4832.2.B454   1987   242   87-14075
ISBN 0-8192-1409-4

In loving memory of the Reverend Canon John Lake Anderson, a faithful priest who saw life with the eyes of a poet. He opened the windows on the fertile landscape of literature, and set my feet on the path which leads to the world of metaphor.

Contents

Foreword

This book is an attempt to express the new (and at the same time very old) ways we find ourselves relating to the contemporary world, and consequently the new ways we are having to seek to communicate our Christian faith about that world. It is written at a time of particular significance for Christians. By the middle of our present century we had exhausted a certain way of relating to the world around us. When we went in search of a new way, we found with some surprise that it involved the recovery of some attitudes and insights which had long been in the scriptures but which Western culture had hidden from us! Consider one such change. Over the last three centuries we human beings have understood ourselves to be observers of the created order from a point outside it. In ways both creative and destructive, we have acted upon that order, changing and adapting it according to our needs (real or imagined). In recent years we have come to realize the complex and sometimes hidden costs of this. At the same time we have begun to capture deep spiritual insights which are very ancient but which have been forgotten or dismissed as irrelevant. Insights of Franciscan, Celtic, Orthodox, and native spirituality converge in this area. All in their own way tell us that our humanity cannot merely be observer and manipulator of creation but must regard itself as within creation. In other words, it is not enough to assemble information about God's creation. We are more and more being called not only to know *about* it as information, but to experience it *intimately* in relationship.

Among our other realizations is the fact that faith can be powerfully communicated by images, symbols, and story. In the rediscovery of symbols and images, now of course dominating our culture through communications technology, we are realizing how powerfully both the Old and New Testaments use image and symbol to communicate faith. We are also, by a real irony, discovering that Judaism, which so rigorously prohibited the making of any graven images, compensated by giving us the world's richest storehouse of verbal images. Finally, we are realizing in our apocalyptic age, full as it is with communications technology spilling out endless images and symbols, that the two great pieces of biblical apocalyptic literature, the book of Daniel in the Old Testament and the book of Revelation in the New, are themselves composed almost entirely of symbols and images. Obviously this communications insight was known some two millenia before the invention of the cathode tube. One is tempted to add that the stained glass window and the icon and the illustrated Celtic gospel were "screens" long before the first television set came to its first living room! In the rediscovery of the story as a communication tool, we are finding again the ability to take scripture from "ordinary" time (the past) and place it in "sacred" time where it is always powerfully "now." Having spoken of these things — image, symbol, story — it is surely cause for our real excitement to realize that these three are precisely the methods used by our Lord Jesus Christ to communicate the things of his kingdom.

Such, and much more, is the stuff of this book. It is an attempt to remind us of things which we ignore at some cost. The irony would be to dismiss its contents as new and thus not to recognize much as being very old. The things of God have an intriguing capacity to remain contemporary!

The Rev'd Dr Herbert O'Driscoll,
rector, Christ Church, Calgary;
former Warden, College of Preachers,
Washington, D.C.

Preface

One of my great pleasures when director of Academic Affairs at the College of Preachers in Washington, D.C., was to meet and converse with the fellows of the college. Of the many with whom I have worked, none showed more passion, wit, seriousness, and vitality than Richard Berryman during his stay as a fellow. Our conversations were extended ones. They were, in fact, *conversations* — which means they were directed by us into areas of mutual interest and consolidating perceptions, the results of which neither of us could imagine prior to our discussions. Richard Berryman graces his correspondents with his probing mind, impatient questioning, and lively imagination.

I am honoured to write a preface for this rather remarkable, though brief, volume. In it are condensed the results of conversations he had with many persons during his fellowship at the college, as well as the results of his commitment to the life of the church as a sustained, and sustaining, dialogue with the sacred. I hope through this book many will find the stimulation for their own contributions to an enquiry within the church which has all but been forgotten in our present obsession with program; namely, program for what?

Canon Berryman's book provides both theoretical and practical grist for the mill for such an enquiry, neither of which can be ignored if the present malaise the church suffers (in consonance with every institution and personage in our late twentieth-century Western world) is to be redressed and the *mysterion* relocated. This relocation will, I believe, take a long time. Many things will accompany it. It will not be completed, if it ever will be completed, perhaps during the lifetime of anyone now alive. This task of relocating the *mysterion* within the *saeculum* involves not only the church. The task is of greater scope than evangelism. It is beyond apologetics. Its importance even transcends theology. It is nothing less than the recovery of mystery without recourse to mystification, and this recovery engages us in an across-the-board re-evaluation of the common sense assumptions by means of which we think.

Canon Berryman is right in affirming that, if a space between ourselves and our modern fate can be achieved, what will appear is an epiphany of the sacred flesh of our existence, incarnate and endowed with dignity. It will be, in short, an epiphany for the wise. But such an epiphany requires, this time, a journey which returns us to ourselves.

R. Taylor Scott
professor of philosophy and religion,
Francis Marion College;
former director of academic affairs,
College of Preachers, Washington, D.C.

Introduction

A world ends when its metaphor has died.

An age becomes an age, all else beside,
When the sensuous poets in their pride invent
Emblems for the soul's consent
That speak the meanings men will never know
But man-imagined images can show.

It perishes when those images, though seen,
No longer mean.

(from "The Metaphor," in *The Human Season* by Archibald MacLeish.
Copyright © 1972 by Archibald MacLeish. Reprinted by permission of
Houghton Mifflin Company.)

Where is the Life we have lost in living?
Where is the wisdom we have lost in knowledge?
Where is the knowledge we have lost in information?

In the vacant places
We will build with new bricks
There are hands and machines
And clay for new brick
And lime for new mortar
Where the bricks are fallen
We will build with new stone
Where the beams are rotten
We will build with new timbers
Where the word is spoken
We will build with new speech

(from Choruses from "*The Rock*"
by T.S. Eliot: Reprinted by permission of Faber and Faber Ltd. from
Collected Poems 1909–1962 by T.S. Eliot.)

The church began with the Word made flesh, the sacred incarnate, embodied in the secular world of human existence. When that Word made flesh created another body, the church, to extend his incarnation until time and secular world would end, his command was to go and communicate. Communication, then, is of the essence of the church's life. When the church communicates poorly, it sickens; when it ceases to communicate, it dies.

This book results from many years of experience in, and thought about, the communication tasks of the church. It comes from a conviction that today, in a world of instant mass-communication, we in the church are not doing that job as well as we could. The reason, I am convinced, is that a whole dimension of communication has been neglected. It is that dimension which goes beyond data sharing into the world of image and sign, of myth and metaphor. This is the world of story and poetry and pre-eminently of scripture. The church today is too much a part of a world in which "those images," of which the poet speaks, those "emblems for the soul's consent . . . though seen, no longer mean." Knowledge, in the biblical sense, is being "lost in information" in both world and church. I am convinced that we do have the "hands and machines" and "clay for new bricks" to build "new speech" — more effective communication in the church and, through it, in the world.

The theological term that describes the entire earthly event of the life of Jesus of Nazareth is *Incarnation*. The life of the church which Jesus formed is sometimes referred to as the extension of the Incarnation. And the day to day existence of the people of God continues to embody (incarnate) his sacred presence in every age. There is a kind of communication which enables that process, enhances it, and makes it plain. I have chosen to call it "incarnational communication." The aim of this book is to assist in reclaiming the ability to communicate in a way that makes sacred presence in human life more plainly seen. Some of what you find here will be familiar; not all of it, of course, will apply in every situation.

There is really little new in this book. It is not primarily a "how-to" manual, though there are many suggestions of things to consider and ways to begin. The purpose is quite simple. It is to open the possibility of regarding our communication task in a new way, by beginning to see our world with new eyes. I think it was Marshall McLuhan who said, "Whoever it was that discovered water, it wasn't a goldfish.'' The fish takes water for granted and never thinks about it. We do the same with the secular world around us; it is simply ''there.''

We have forgotten what is so plain in the scriptures — that it is in the depths of daily experience that we find the sacred. It is in bushes which burn and are not consumed, clouds which lead by day and give way to pillars of fire by night; in sowers, seeds, and patches on threadbare garments; in lost coins and runaway youth; and ultimately in the most solidly secular of stuff — water, wine, and broken bread. Let us immerse ourselves in that stuff of our world, and thereby find meaning in our emblems and new speech in our words made flesh.

Acknowledgements

This book began a long time ago, and many people and experiences contributed to it. It would not finally have come to fruition without a space of time in which to write it and the guidance and support of certain individuals in recent days. It is impossible to list all who have contributed to this, the end result of more than thirty years of learning and living.

I would be remiss, however, if I did not acknowledge my deep indebtedness to, and express my most sincere gratitude for, the patience, wisdom, and inspiration of the late Canon John Lake Anderson; the enlightened, enabling sabbatical policy of the General Synod of the Anglican Church of Canada; and a generous sabbatical grant.

I am very conscious of the dedicated work of other members of the staff of the national office of the Anglican Church, especially those in communications, who picked up the slack while I was on sabbatical, adding to their already overly busy lives.

I was truly overwhelmed by the admirable facilities and staff of the College of Preachers and the National Cathedral in Washington, D.C., and their generosity in granting me a Resident Fellowship at the college to make use of those precious resources, and by the remarkable brilliance and insight and the deep, abiding friendship of the Rev Dr R. Taylor Scott, former director of Academic Affairs at the College of Preachers.

Finally, but most deeply, I thank Christine, Anne, Mary, Susan, and Stephen who loved me through the wilderness.

1
Thoughts on a
University Convocation, 1985

I recently attended the graduation of my son from university. Convocation programs are great social barometers; they identify the high and low pressure areas in our societal environment. In Stephen's humanities faculty, out of 249 Bachelor of Arts degrees, only 12 were philosophy majors — that is, 4%. In the science faculty, out of 234 Bachelors, a total of 97 had majored in computer science or mathematics — about 41%. What is more, the remaining 59% were divided among nine other separate disciplines.

The other notable feature of the convocation program was the list of those to be admitted Doctors of Philosophy and the titles of their dissertations, their specialties. Here are two examples: "Associative Interactions Between Septo-dentate and Perforant Path Afferent to the Rat Dentate Gyrus" and "Quasi Two Dimensional Magnetic Properties of the Tri-Rutile Phases MTa_2O_6, M = V, Fe, Co, Ni."

These random observations of one convocation at a single Canadian university certainly are not sufficient to prove anything, but they do give some food for thought. They said to me that it is a time in which valued knowledge is data about the physical world. I was conscious that I was seeing the young adults of a world which *does* much more than it *thinks* about the implications of its actions. I felt confirmation of a nagging suspicion that this is an age of specialists, specialists who can barely, if at all, talk to each other across the isolating boundaries of their increasingly exotic disciplines. It seems that more and more of our ability to communicate is governed by what can be translated into computer language and by the compatability of our "hardware." The computer programmer has become the scribe of our society! The implications of this alarm me. Whatever those scribes cannot translate may casually be dismissed as unimportant — it does not matter; that is, it "has no matter," it does not exist.

Where did such a world come from? How did it evolve while I wasn't looking? Is it as different from previous worlds as it feels to me? What effect will it, or does it now, have on me? The world in which we live is sometimes referred to as "modern" or "scientific." It is crucial that we grasp the reason why it is also known, by some, as a Cartesian world. This title honours the French philosopher Renée Descartes, who lived from 1596 to 1650 on the frontier of a new world-view. That view shaped and formed the physical reality we now see around us and in the deep reaches of space. It can truly be said that Descartes and his contemporaries took the first steps towards Neil Armstrong's "great step for humanity" onto the surface of the moon. Descartes' famous "Cogito, ergo sum" ("I think, therefore I am") led him to construct a total philosophical system which changed the way humanity saw itself and the universe. From the primeval mists to the dawning of Descartes' seventeenth century, humankind had experienced itself as part of the world in which it lived. But Cartesian philosophy and the advent of literacy, at least in Europe, began to alter that radically. The availability of printed books, and an increasingly literate public to acquire them, contributed to the rapid dissemination of new ideas. The Protestant Reformation blazed as flame in dry stubble across Europe as a result. Even more important, however, humankind's way of perceiving the world was vastly altered.

Before the alphabet was invented, pre-literate humanity lived in what is sometimes referred to as an "acoustic" world. A world of the ear primarily, and of all the senses in conjunction — an all-at-once perception of the evironment. Reality was experienced simultaneously by sight, hearing, touch, smell, and taste without discrimination. Time and space were a great surrounding continuum for our ancestors. In such an environment sung poetry was the mass media, and oral story telling was the link with people's history. Then came the printed word. Knowledge of, and relationship with, the world increasingly depended on the little black marks of the alphabet, running in ordered sequence across a page. The audible, pictorial, tactile, and olfactory encounter with the environment was squeezed into the visual and, more critically, the abstract. But these black marks you are now perceiving have, of themselves, no intrinsic meaning. They are quite arbitrary abstract markings, chosen and accepted to "stand for" meaning. Reality is now perceived not all at once but one black mark at a time — segmented, sequential, fragmented along a straight line. My perception of reality is no longer mine alone; it is universal, repeatable, ordered. Once I am programmed in early years to accept a view of reality which says, "When I see it in black and white, I'll believe it," it is almost impossible for me to think in a clearly independent, subjective manner about my world ever again, without conscious effort.

What happens to your view of your world when, as a child, you accept that letters have sounds? From then on verbal images will accompany your thoughts. You, from that point on, will live in a different world from that inhabited by illiterate persons. Discuss, as I have, with those in the church who today work among non-literate aboriginal peoples. Translation involves far more than language; it requires entering another world. When Christian missionaries invent script for previously non-literate people, they do more than bring a religious message and a literature, they create a new world for those people. I wish I could feel easier about that, or not quite so dismayed with what frequently results from that process.

How you understand who you are and what is real around you is of the deepest significance in the life of a human. It governs all your relationships. I take *understand* here in its root meaning of "knowing your position in relation to," "knowing where you stand." In this sense print, literacy, and Descartes (with a few of his friends) changed forever our understanding of ourselves and our surroundings. The world became entirely a thing of cause and effect, of lineal progression, and something external to me *of which I am not a part.* The world (and, therefore, another person) became something "out there." Knowledge became information *about* things and people, gathered and recorded, a fact at a time. The long journey to "bits" of data, the word processor, and the computer had begun.

Obviously this did not cause humans to lose their sense of touch, smell, taste, hearing, and sight. We continue all these sensate activities, but the world about which they tell us became suspect. Descartes declared, "Whatever I had admitted until now as most true I took in either from the senses or through the senses;

however, I noticed that they sometimes deceived me. And it is a mark of prudence never to trust wholly in those things which have once deceived us."[1] From such simple beginnings comes a computerized world.

When knowledge became "information *about*" and was accepted as the only kind of knowledge which mattered, all human experience that could not be categorized, analyzed, specified, and translated into data was trivialized. That is our heritage from Descartes. That is what Eliot means by "the knowledge we have lost in information." In that world, "knowledge about" is power. For example, many, if not most, people who live in urban areas and work for even a small business or corporation, are paid in information about themselves. Their employer gives information about them to their bank's computer, which stores it in its memory bank. The employee can then go into a store and, with a piece of plastic, exchange some of that information for merchandise. No money is involved, only information. We need no further proof of the awesome power of "information about" than the insanely expensive "spy in the sky" satellite programs of the major nations. The more you know about your enemy, or supposed enemy, the less danger he is to you and the more power you have over him.

The other thing which loses out in the power struggle for importance in a Cartesian world is language and the thought which it embodies. As George Steiner points out, between all verbal languages there exists always the possibility of at least rough equivalents. It has always been possible to translate from one to another. This is not so with the "grammar" of higher mathematics. Steiner refers to "a new, rich, complex and dynamic language which is progressively intranslatable." He adds, "The most decisive change in Western (intellectual) life since the 17th Century is the submission of successively larger areas of knowledge to the modes and proceedings of mathematics. . . . You cannot translate, paraphrase or find an equivalent in verbal speech for the properties of n-dimensional manifolds."[2] (Look again at the second PhD dissertation I mention above!)

The language which suffers most, and eventually dies in such a world, is the language of metaphor. This book is, above all else, an attempt to provide at least some life-support systems for that dying patient. Let us heed again the warning of Archibald MacLeish.

A world ends when its metaphor has died.

An age becomes an age, all else beside.
When the sensuous poets, in their pride invent,
Emblems for the soul's consent,
That speak the meanings men will never know,
But man-imagined images can show.

It perishes when those images, though seen,
No longer mean.

(from "The Metaphor")

We live in that world which could, quite literally, die if we cannot give life to its metaphors. I believe the way to give meaning, and therefore life, back to those images which "though seen, no longer mean," is to begin to grapple with this world, this time, this place in which we live. Recall that "this world, time, and place" is the literal meaning of the Latin word *saeculum*. So we begin with the secular. We must take seriously the world of the senses, whether it occasionally deceives the Decartes who inhabit it or not. We must become better at perceiving the sacred in the secular, and at translating that perception into "such a Language and Order as is most easy and plain for the understanding" of God's people (to borrow from the recommendations of the Prayer Book of 1552).

2
The Things in Life
that Really Count

A few Christmases ago the largest department store chain in Canada used a catchy jingle in its TV advertising which urged us, "For the things in life that really count, just say, 'Charge it' on your Eaton's account." This implies that those parts of our *saeculum*, our total environment, that matter, that have ultimate reality, are purchasable. (We note again that they can be obtained by providing information about oneself with a plastic card which gives access to a computer memory bank.) We dismiss this advertising gimmick as trivial at our peril. It is a telling example of how deeply ingrained in our collective psyche is the Cartesian world view. The writers of TV advertising rely on it to make their impact.

This commercial gave me the same uneasy feeling I have when I see "mainline" religious programming on local cable TV or on the commercial networks. With very few exceptions, most of what is produced is information about the life and/or teachings of the church. To be sure, sometimes the visual presentation is enhanced by slides or actuality footage or the taping of "real" people discussing in a studio; but the end is virtually always the same — giving information about something. This, I am convinced, is only partly due to lack of funds, professional experience, or personnel. Even when these are available, the end result is data, sometimes very visual data, but nontheless data — "information about."

It is our acceptance of the Cartesian world view that makes us rely primarily on print for communication in the church. "I want to see it in print" is the test of authenticity constantly demanded. "Let me see it in black and white" is no idle request. As a producer of audio-visual resources for the church, I am all too familiar with the suspicion attached to productions which rely primarily on the visual. They are too indefinite, too ill-defined; they lack the data we crave. Therefore, most audio-visuals acceptable to church committees are heavily informational and are usually accompanied by copious print materials. Those which use several media and require a more holistic or feeling response are dismissed as "too slick." They run counter to our conventional wisdom, they create demands on us that make us vaguely uneasy, they ask us to relate to our knowledge in a different way. In this they illustrate how tied we are to a world of, what William Blake called, "Newton's sleep." They require us to recall the "knowledge we have lost in information," as Eliot describes it.

I must add a caveat here before I proceed any further. There is no question that Descartes' beginnings have led us to a world with much less disease, with the potential (though not yet the will) to feed adequately every human on earth, with the possibility of sharing data information which could truly create a "global village." I do not need to add my voice to the thousands who remind us, however, that there is a demonic side to all that potential which indeed threatens us daily with extinction. The ability to communicate instantaneously is now here. Word processors, computers, telephone modums, satellite up and down links are facts of our daily existence and commerce, whether we personally make use of them or not. The church is beginning to look seriously at the potential of all that electronic hard and soft-ware to make her sharing of information and educational endeavours more efficient and better able to serve a much more worthy enterprise than the selling of autos or the predicting of stock-market swings or election results.

I hasten to say that I am in the front ranks of the crowd that stands and cheers such efforts at all levels of our church system. However, I also stand to cry aloud that such communication primarily serves systems, it does not create community. We could well find ourselves with an information system as splendid as any possessed by a corporation of similar size, but as hollow as it is splendid, and as empty of the sacred as it is full of data. I believe there is a growing awareness, at least at the parish level, that there is something lacking in the way we communicate in the church. Is it too trite to say we are beginning to feel that our communications efforts have lost their soul? I am convinced that we are seeing a contemporary application of Christ's question in the Sermon on the Mount: "Who will offer his son a stone when he asks for bread?" The bread the community of the church seeks is an encounter with the sacred and with each other; the stone too often offered is information about systems, be they organizational or doctrinal. So, proceed with the purchase and use of your personal computer with word processor capabilities, and your telephone modum, but do not think when it is fully operational that you will thereby be communicating fully. There is more to "word-processing" for those who believe in the Word made flesh.

There is another contemporary phenomenon in church life which, at one and the same time, illustrates how we are enslaved in Descartes' world and yet capable of breaking out of it — in fact, yearning to do so. Television has made us a much more visually oriented society; it has created in us a craving for the visual. One result in the life certainly of the Anglican church, but to some extent in all the mainline churches, is quite remarkable. This is especially so in that it has happened quietly, peacefully, and with virtually no comment. I refer to the explosion of visual accompaniments to our worship. Banners hang from the church walls and are carried high in procession. Processions are elaborate, no longer mere movement of the choir to their accustomed position during the first hymn. Candles adorn altars and flicker from tapers borne in the hands of colourfully robed acolytes. Clergy lay aside sombre black cassocks and plain surplices in favour of albs and hand crafted stoles of every conceivable hue and decorative appliqué. Chasubles, copes, and choir gowns blossom in shades from violet to vermillion. And congregations love it! They crave it! And, what is more, no questions are asked about "What does it mean?"

That is the change. When I was in seminary thirty years ago, every visual, external action, movement, or garment used in worship was scrutinized excruciatingly; they meant something, indicated something, and gave clues to what was called the "churchmanship" of priest or parish. Woe to any young priest who deviated from the parish norm. I can recall serious discussions about how much white collar one allowed to show in the slot in front of one's black clerical stock — the wider the white, the "lower" one's churchmanship. The tone of church life and worship in an entire diocese could be ascertained by a glance at the ecclesiastical haberdashery of its bishop! In today's TV world that all is regarded as quaint archaic behaviour of a bygone era. This, we may thankfully declare, is a small chink in Cartesian armour. However, such visual accompaniment to worship, including movement and colour and texture, seems in most cases haphazard. When we examine later in detail the ingredients of ritual as a way of encountering the sacred in the secular, we will consider how they might be used in a more deliberate and therefore more meaningful manner.

There is little room in a Cartesian world for a God to whom we are called to relate with all "our heart and soul and mind and strength." It is a world empty of what Rudolph Otto calls the "Numinous," the "Wholly Other." Given the all-pervasiveness of the data-centred environment in which we now live, can we hope still to encounter a sacred presence within the stuff of daily life? The alternative, I believe, is to stare blankly into a universe empty of all but sterile impersonal laws of physics. That would be a black hole in which the music of the spheres has been replaced by a truly total "dead silence." I cannot help but think that a deep-rooted fear of just such a universe lies behind the current flooding of the movie market with films about extra-terrestrials. It is also noteworthy that such movies have begun recently to feature lovable aliens such as *E.T.* and *Cocoon*, rather than terrifying science-fiction monsters. Could a chillingly lonely Cartesian world be the reason that *E.T.* was seen by more people and grossed more money in one year than any movie in history, regardless of how long it ran? We are quite literally afraid of the world in which we live, for we know to be alone in it is to die. We realize deep inside that, like E.T., we also will shrivel and perish without a relationship to "the Other."

There are ways to seek life-giving relationships which do not fade when the lights come on in the theatre. We need to ask how we might see and know the world around us in a different way, so as to encounter the God who is both beyond and incarnate. We begin our journey back into a world of sacred, nourishing encounters by probing what the scriptures mean when they talk about "knowing" God and the created order.

3
And Adam
Knew his Wife

"Knowing" in the Old Testament implies a personal relationship between the one who knows and the thing or person known. This is obviously more readily grasped when the object known is a person. It is difficult to imagine a personal relationship with a rock. If we were to think, rather, in terms of *understanding* that rock, a relationship would seem less incredible. That is, if we accept *understand* to convey knowing "where you stand" in relation to something. To know an inanimate object in the Old Testament is to apprehend the "whatness" of it and, in knowing it, to understand its place in our *saeculum*, our immediate, intimate personal environment. Our relationship to it, as well, may be part of something far greater. Israel's relationship to Mount Sinai was also its relationship to Yahweh, whose presence they encountered on its slopes. The Red Sea was not merely a body of water; it was the Exodus event. This does not necessarily imply having a scientific, data-filled knowledge of such an inanimate thing. It is more a realization of the effect of the object on our lives, and our possible effect on it. We should note, however, that this scriptural sense of knowing does not preclude a scientifically detailed knowledge; I am sure many astronomers know space in a way I never shall.

Sometimes this kind of knowledge is obtained by experience. For example, to know afflictions can be a way of knowing God and being known by him. The Old Testament speaks of knowing loss of children, and of knowing disease, grief, joy, or God's vengeance. However, the very fact that the Hebrew can, and does frequently, speak of the sexual union of man and woman as "knowing" indicates that knowledge is far more than simply being aware of something or someone's existence. Certainly such knowledge goes beyond merely possessing information about another person — height, weight, colour of eyes, and hair. This knowledge is an activity which involves the whole individual, not simply the conscious, data-processing, rational mind.

When one starts to talk about that kind of knowledge, it is almost impossible to avoid sexual language: "Now Adam knew his wife"; "And the two shall be as one." Knowing a person in the biblical sense means you can never again step back and be entirely separate again. This is the kind of knowledge of world and person which our ancestors were able to obtain simultaneously in an all-at-once comprehension by ear, eye, touch, feel, and smell. We, in our arrogance or blindness, call that primitive, and yet there are peoples in the world today who can still approach their environment in that fashion; and we might well learn from them before they too lose their knowledge in information overload. To know the world in that fundamental way means that I experience myself as being fully in it and part of it, not a separate observer of it. I enter it and it penetrates me. This is a very sensual way of perceiving that involves my total being. Further, this kind of knowing is always accompanied by an emotional reaction. How I relate to someone or something can make me grieve or rejoice, love or hate. It may also cause me to become something other than what I was. The relationship implied by such knowledge manifests itself in action, in being, which corresponds to that relationship. A striking example of this is in Isaiah 1:3.

The ox knows its owner, and the ass its master's stall; but Israel, my own people, has no knowledge, no discernment.

The chapter continues, in graphic detail, to describe how Israel's lack of knowledge is not theological illiteracy, but a failure to practise its required relationship to God, and how this has adversely affected its very nature as a people.

Perhaps the best known example of this approach to knowledge is in the second and third chapters of Genesis. The command to Adam and Eve is to avoid the "tree of the knowledge of good and evil." The serpent declares to them the reason: to eat of the fruit would make them "like gods, knowing both good and evil." In this, as in most scripture stories, the choice of words is seldom accidental. To transgress this command will not result in mere empirical or even theological knowledge — not in data about good and evil. It will, rather, allow them fully to experience what wrong *is*, because their relationship to it will have changed. They will not so much *know* evil as they will *be* evil. When the Old Testament approaches the question of knowing God, it consistently refers to the quality of a person's relationship to God. Wherever today's Christian might use words such as *believe* or *faith*, the Old Testament employs some form of the phrase *to know God*. Knowledge of God originates through an encounter with God in the same way that knowledge of any other person is derived.

There is, as well, a reciprocal nature to this encounter. In the drama of the people of God, God teaches human persons, searches and tests them. It is through a recognition of God's activity in the events of one's life that one gains the knowledge of oneself as related to him. This results in a concrete, existential awareness of what it means to have a God, and of what sort of person this requires one to become. The entire fourth chapter of Proverbs, for example, is virtually a song of celebration of this kind of knowledge. This insistence on effective action stemming from knowledge saves the Hebraic concept from mere sentimentalism. Though knowledge of God results in "fear" of him, it is not a cowering, emotional response so much as a respect of the majesty and power which is shown in becoming what God would have one be. Here is exemplified the huge gulf separating the Greek (and Cartesian) view of knowledge from the Hebraic. For the Greek, knowledge is primarily theoretical. It is a matter of one's own discretion whether that knowledge results in any particular conduct or other. Pure contemplation of the nature of God is a Greek activity. For the Hebrew, the immediate response to an encounter with the divine is, "How fearsome is this place! This is no other than the house of God, this is the gate of heaven" (Gen 28:17).

A final aspect of this Old Testament view of knowledge which is important to consider, is that the God of the Old Testament is a God who wants to be known. Primarily the Old Testament records revelations to chosen persons. However, there is never any doubt that personal, individual knowledge of (relationship to) God is given in order that it might be extended, so that all may come to know him. "This is the covenant which I will make with Israel after those days, says the Lord; I will set my law within them and write it on their hearts; I will become their God and they shall become my people. No longer need they teach one another to know the Lord; all of them, high and low alike, shall know me, says the Lord'' (Jer 31:33–34). No finer description may be found of the kind of knowledge which may yet reclaim a world of effective metaphor for today's church. It is in this self-revelatory nature of God that we must begin the quest.

4
A God
Who Wants
To Be Known

As Christians we say we believe in a God who communicates. Not only does God communicate in the sense of conveying, by a variety of means, information about his being, nature, and will to his people; but, we also say, God *acts* by communicating. In the drama of the people of Israel in the Old Testament, very seldom do we read, "And God did . . ." More often it is, "And God said . . ." and something came about. When I say "star" to you, an image of a bright object in the sky is conveyed to your mind. When God says "star," a twinkling light appears in the heavens where before there had been only darkness. He says, "Let there be light," and there is light! We go so far as to claim that God "calls" each of us into existence. It is no semantic accident that the ultimate self-revelation of God in the Christian faith is referred to as the "Word made flesh." The writer of the fourth gospel is making a basic statement about the communicative nature of God's interaction with the world and the people he had created.

The other remarkable distinction we observe in the scriptural accounts of this communicating God's not infrequent interventions into human history, is that his methods are very much of a non-Cartesian nature. To put it simply, they are what we usually call "audio-visuals" which appeal to the all-at-oneness of the senses. This should not come as a surprise; these events occurred in a pre-literate world whose inhabitants would simply expect to encounter the sacred in the same manner that they experienced everything else in daily life. So God's communications come in pillars of cloud by day and of fire by night, in burning bushes and chariots, in ladders set up to heaven, in night visions and shining stars, and in the living calm at the eye of the hurricane. The birth pangs of the Christian community which we call the church were accompanied by rushing winds and flames of fire and language which overcame the Babel barriers to communication.

In our sophisticated, scientific society such fabulous, seemingly super-natural happenings are to some embarrassing and to others a real stumbling block, preventing acceptance of anything the church teaches. The problem lies in treating such phenomena as events, rather than as halting, poetic attempts to describe awesome, deeply personal human experiences. The difficulty in interpreting such evidences of God's involvement in human lives comes from applying a Cartesian model of knowing to an all-at-once encounter with the sacred in the secular.

St Paul refers to such experiences as *mysterion tou theou*, the "mystery of God." This is a tantalizing concept which Paul, rabbinic scholar that he was, picked up and embellished from the Septuagint, the Greek version of the Old Testament. I say "tantalizing" because it illustrates so well the idea of a God who wants to be known, who plans, even schemes, so that his people will encounter him. The literal meaning of *mysterion* is "confidential speech or advice, particularly that of the king, kept hidden until conditions are in place for disclosure to a circle of confidants." What a delightful image for the God we may know and encounter! This is no animistic deity found in a generalized way in spirits of rocks, trees, and sunsets. This is a personal, communicative creator, involved in and having a plan for creation.

Paul describes God's *mysterion* as prepared before the world was (1 Cor 2:7) concealed from the aeons (Eph 3:9, Rom 16:25) hidden in God the creator of all things (Eph 3:9) and, of course, fully revealed in Jesus, the Christ, whom he (Paul) has encountered on the road to Damascus. "It was by a revelation that his *mystery* was *made known* to me . . . you may perceive that I *understand* the *mystery* of Christ. In former generations this was not disclosed to the human race; but now it has been revealed by inspiration to his dedicated apostles and prophets" (Eph 3:3–5). It was hidden for long ages in God the creator of the universe, in order that now, through the church , the wisdom of God in all its varied forms might be made known to the rulers and authorities in the realms of heaven. A classic, text-book definition of the Septuagint meaning of *mysterion*, sprinkled throughout with words we have already seen as pregnant with significance for the Old Testament.

The early church expanded the dimensions of *mysterion*. The basic events of salvation in the Incarnation itself — Christ's birth, miracles, teachings, death, resurrection, and ascension — continue to be referred to as *mysterion*. However, now are included such Old Testament figures and events as have typological significance. Moses lifting up the fiery serpent in the wilderness, the slaying of the Passover lamb, the descriptions of the servant "despised and rejected of men" in Isaiah — these are seen as allegorical foreshadowings of the mysteries of the Logos of God.

It is unfortunate for us that, when the scriptures were translated from Greek to Latin, the word *mysterion* was translated *"sacramentum."* This was a legalistic term denoting the oath of allegiance required of a soldier on entering the Roman army. Although that meaning has interesting connotations for baptism as an entrance into the church militant, it also has a formalizing rigidity. It sounds, and is, official. Not surprisingly, as the church developed, the term *sacrament* came to be restricted to a set number of institutionalized actions primarily associated with rites of passage. At the very least this suggests that encounters with the sacred are limited to such occasions. *Mysterion* — a universal plan of divine self-revelation — becomes *sacramentum*, official, narrow, predictable — no longer an expected, hoped-for event which could happen around the next bend in the road, or at the next brilliantly blossomed bush.

This is not, in any way, meant to detract from the sacraments in today's church, or to deny their validity as encounters with the sacred in the secular. They are outward, visible signs (in our *saeculum*) of inward, spiritual grace — encounters with the divine action of God. However, if we look only to such acts as examples of *mysterion*, we have emptied a significant concept concerning divine self-communication of its full potential for our day. Throughout the remainder of this work we will endeavour to find, to recover, means of detecting God's *mysterion* in a variety of ways in our midst. Do not expect him to be any less versatile in his methods than he has been in the past. This is the heart of what I choose to call "incarnational communication."

The key to this approach to communication in the church lies in the fact that *mysterion* begins with God. There is a magnificent example of this in an incident described in the book of Isaiah.

The people of Israel once again murmur against their leaders. Their teachings do not satisfy. They are not what they are looking for. "Perhaps," someone says, "the prophets in Egypt, with all their exotic sophistication, will have the answers we seek." Isaiah confronts the people with an image of their God which is at once breathtaking in its simplicity and yet strikingly profound. "The Lord," he declares, "waits to be gracious to you." Once again we encounter the God who wants to be known, not in information about his nature or will but simply in a gracious, personal relationship. Isaiah continues, "Your teacher will not hide himself anymore, but your eyes shall see your teacher. And your ears shall hear a word behind you, saying, 'This is the way, walk in it'" (Is 30:18). Is this not a moving description of a God who waits patiently to reveal himself to his people when they are prepared to open themselves to the relationship? As a trusted friend he will walk behind them as they seek their way in the wilderness, whispering in their ear, "No, not that path my friend, over here. This is the way, come along with me."

We must recover that exciting, spontaneous, anticipatory sense of *mysterion*. There are clues available in the scriptures, the life of the church, and the language we call metaphor which will help us to do so.

5
A Star
in the East

"We observed the rising of his star, and we have come to pay him homage" (Matt 2:2). This announces the arrival of those mysterious visitors from the east. The magi suddenly appear on the stage of history and exit as quickly as they came, leaving us with an annual festival in the church year — the Epiphany, the manifestation of the Christ Child to the gentiles. We may regret that a word from the church's heritage has been thus "frozen," and emptied of its potential in normal use. *Epiphany* has come to mean 6 January or at most, in more traditional observances, that day and its octave. True, the Greek *epiphanos* means "to manifest, show forth, make clear." Equally, the visit of the non-Jewish magi did make clear, or manifest, that this "news . . . great joy . . . in the city of David a deliverer has been born" was news for the whole world, not merely a long-awaited Jewish messiah (Luke 2:12). However, to restrict this term to one event, no matter how meaningful, is to lose a great deal.

The word *epiphany* used to have no such limitation. The lections provided for the Sundays in the liturgical Epiphany season presented a series of "epiphanies," such as the changing of water into wine at the wedding feast in Cana of Galilee and the healing of a (Roman) centurion's servant, which illustrated differing aspects of the nature of this Jesus born in Bethlehem. *Revelations, insights* they were as well, but these words seem to lack something of the power of epiphany. An epiphany is as if, for a fleeting moment, some action, some person, some event caused curtains to part and we received a sudden, swift glimpse into the total reality of a situation. It is a super-charged instant which may have layer upon layer of meaning and implication. An epiphany is, in the strict sense of the word, a supernatural event which involves natural things.

There are at least two important elements to bear in mind about epiphanies. First, they originate with God. The direction of the communication is towards us; epiphany is one of the tools in the hands of the self-revealing God. Second, the "stuff" of epiphanies is found in the *saeculum,* the ordinary here and now. They are supernatural only in the sense that they are charged with more content than by nature they would normally contain.

The term *epiphany* is not entirely theological or liturgical. Irish writer James Joyce, for example, used it to describe highly significant encounters with seemingly insignificant things which totally changed his perspective, his way of seeing things, and eventually the course of his life. One such incident is described in the autobiographical sketch of his early years.

"He drained his third cup of watery tea to the dregs and set to chewing the crusts of fried bread that were scattered near him, staring into the dark pool of the jar. The yellow dripping had been scooped out like a boghole, and the pool under it brought back to his memory the dark turfcoloured water of the bath in Clongowes."[3] The jar of greasy bacon drippings symbolized for him the totality of his stifling environment of grinding poverty and sterile ugliness from which his whole being ached to be delivered, into a world of art and beauty and truth. What to others was the most common daily fare of a poor Irish household, was to the young Joyce a fleeting epiphanic vision of the reality of his existence.

Moses' bush and magi's star, Paul's Damascus road and the bread broken at Emmaus have become, through association with scripture story and liturgical observance, holy things. They have ceased to be part of our *saeculum,* and we forget that they were part of the stuff of the lives of those involved. Perhaps James Joyce's jar of drippings will bring closer to home the essential truth that epiphanies take place in the midst of "the trivial round, the common task." Ability to see epiphanies is the ability to see supercharged reality and hear the active word of God speaking through the mundane. In Isaiah's image, it is to hear God whispering in your ear.

Obviously this does not happen to everyone. Moses stopped and frantically began to tear off his sandals. But I wonder how many other desert nomadic herdsmen passed the *loranthus acaciae* bush, the crimson-flowered mistletoe (whose nickname, even today among those same herdsmen, is "burning bush") and did nothing more than comment on how its petals were so brilliant that you could almost imagine they were flames. The magi tracked the star to its source. But how many millions of eyes glanced at the skies of the Middle East and remarked about the brightness of that one star? Certainly on the road to Damascus as Saul the persecutor was confronted by the risen Christ, "the men who were travelling with him . . . heard the voice, but could see no one" (Acts 9:7).

I would like to retell those familar stories, not because we should expect epiphanies in our lives to match their intensity, but because in them the basic ingredients of epiphany are so clear. In each of them we observe someone in deep mental turmoil, grappling with the reality of the situation. There is much musing on the events happening around them — a seeking of patterns, a looking for order in the confusion of life.

Moses had fled Egypt, having struck down and killed one of the cruel Egyptian concentration camp guards. Later he had found a new life, an adoptive family, and a wife and son. Yet, as he sat meditatively watching his sheep or wandering aimlessly with them from one meagre grazing patch to the next, his mind returned constantly to Israel, his and God's people in Egypt. How were they? Would there ever be deliverance for them? Had Jehovah-God really deserted them? Had he no power among the gods of Pharaoh? It took only one glance at the bush's flaming petals to drive him to his sandal straps, as the voice echoing his own thoughts declared, "I have indeed seen the misery of my people in Egypt. I have heard their outcry . . . I have taken heed of their sufferings . . . Come now; I will send you to Pharaoh and you shall bring my people Israel out of Egypt" (Exod 3:7 –10).

For ages the magi, as the ruling, priestly caste of their Zoroastrian society, were well versed in the astrological secrets of the skies. Each segment of the heavenly canopy was designated for one of the known nations around them. So when a brilliant new star suddenly appeared in that part of the heavens assigned to the Hebrews, they knew where their search for its meaning must lie. Even as they began their inquiry into the sacred writings of the Israelites, they began their journey. Their final questioning of the learned men of Herod's court gave them their ultimate clue and pointed them to Bethlehem. Few epiphanies had as thorough a mental preparation as the one which originally gave us the term and entitled their visit for all time.

"Meanwhile Saul was still breathing murderous threats against the disciples of the Lord" (Acts 9:1). Saul, the young rising star of the Sanhedrin (the first century version of the hard-nosed special investigator), was making quite a name in rabbinical circles as the one who would rid them of this new sectarian nuisance, the Christians. He had been there when Stephen was smashed into oblivion by the stones of a heretic's execution. He even held the coats of the sweating stone throwers and heard the handsome young man with "the face of an angel," cry his last words, "Lord, do not hold this sin against them" (Acts 7:60).

Now, riding slowly along the road to Damascus, where he knew there was another lot of these followers of Jesus simply asking to share Stephen's fate with their open preaching and blasphemy, he pondered. What was it about them? No matter how he and the authorities persecuted them they never fought back. In calm confidence they spoke of a Lord who had conquered all the pain the world had to offer, even death itself. The next thing he knew, he was on his knees trying to shield his eyes from the most blinding, searing flash imaginable, confronted by a Person and a voice. The flash of Saul's epiphany was St Paul's natal star.

A final example. Perhaps, in its simplicity, the clearest one for us today. Two men, dejected to the point of despair, trudge home towards Emmaus from Jerusalem and its recent trauma. In one week end the dreams of three years had been shattered in the grotesquely broken body of their friend and Master. It was not merely the death of a friend. It was the extinguishing of a flame of hope kindled generations ago in Israel and carefully nutured until it had flared to life in the person and teachings of Jesus of Nazareth. They had been so sure that he was the one promised for so long. Now all that was finished.

They are overtaken by a stranger in the dusk, who inquires of their sadness. They find it difficult to believe that anyone could not have heard of the events of the past months, and especially of the last week. But they tell him. They illustrate from their limited knowledge of scripture, but more vividly from their own experience, why they were so sure. They even add the quite preposterous story that some of the women disciples had seen the Master alive after his burial. Oddly enough, the stranger adds even more scriptural evidence to their own. If anything, he gives more credence to their hope — their now devasted hope.

Home at last! Would the stranger join them for a simple meal and a night's rest on his journey? Out of common courtesy they ask him to say the traditional blessing of their table and break the bread. Break it he does, and suddenly the despair is burned out of their hearts in the fire of divine love, and life for them is irrevocably changed. The scriptures were there, the experience was there, even Christ's presence was with them; but the epiphany occurs in the basic stuff of their lives — the breaking of bread at a simple meal at a peasant's table.

It seems then, that epiphanies happen to those who have prepared the way with conscious contemplation. There seems to be a struggling to uncover the activity of God in their own individual *saeculum,* in the here and now of their personal world. They may not see the whole panorama of divine activity, but by sharing their encounter of the sacred in the secular with others in community, they experience a growing awareness of the divine activity. So, as part of our rediscovery of incarnational communication, we must begin to expect epiphanies. We must work with those who tell us about them. Certainly, not all will be as spectacular as Martin Luther King's dream or Mother Teresa's vision of Christ in the faces of the dying destitute on the streets of Calcutta, but we must learn to identify those occasions when our communicating God speaks to us in the ordinariness of our lives.

My good friend and all too infrequent mentor, Herbert O'Driscoll, in his recent autobiographical memoir, *A Doorway in Time,* states this with his usual poetic beauty: "Scripture . . . introduces us to the endless sequence of men and women who do see God. Perhaps one should say that they see God as Crusoe saw the marks of another human footprint in the sand of his hitherto solitary island. So the footprint of the passing God is discerned in daily experience, in the events of private and public history, in the glory and terror of nature, and in the mystery and complexity of human encounter and relationship. . . .

"The common attitude of so many lives in the Bible is this ability to see signs. The simple word *sign* gives us the word *significance* and that is essentially the quest I speak of, the discerning of significance in daily experience. Among the few expressions of exasperation we hear from our Lord are those in which he expresses regret at the inability of some to see signs of God's activity in the things happening around them."[4]

Let me close this description of epiphany with a personal experience. Early in my pastoral ministry I was spending a particularly cold winter's afternoon visiting parish families in my small, less than affluent area. It had been an especially frustrating several hours. The people I had wanted to see were not at home. I was becoming more chilled by the minute, and I really began to wonder if this was what I had spent so much time and effort preparing for in seminary. "Is this what ministry is all about?" I wondered as I turned my car towards home and warmth and a cup of coffee. Suddenly, without even knowing why, I pulled over to the side of the road and heard a voice (if it was my own, to this day I do not know) saying, "You must go and visit Mrs Warburton." Mrs Warburton. She lived in abject poverty in a shack in the midst of a slum area, and virtually no one but me cared whether she lived or died. I had visited her and given her communion a few days before, and I found myself echoing Moses' list of perfectly legitimate reasons why I need not go. But I knew I must go.

As I stamped my frigid feet on her front step, I noticed she was peering out of the filthy window to the side of the door and glancing down at the small fuel oil tank just below it. She admitted me to her one small room, which was only slightly warmer than the blustery world outside. When I inquired why she did not turn up her little oil burner, she replied, "I've run out of oil."

"You will be dead by morning," I exclaimed. She explained that the oil company would not deliver such a small, single delivery load. Taking a five-gallon can from her porch, I hurried off to the nearest service station and returned shortly with enough oil to see her through the night, and assurance that more oil would arrive in the morning. Turning to me with a look which will be with me to the grave, she quietly said, "It's funny, you know. Whenever I pray for something, you show up with it."

An empty oil drum on a cold afternoon outside a widow's shack was an epiphany containing all the knowledge there will ever be in me of what pastoral ministry is all about.

6
Tell Me
the Old, Old Story

Part of the expectation of epiphany is the acceptance of the presence, in this here and now, of a God who wishes to be known. Such acceptance is nurtured by feeding on the stories of God's activity in the past. These constitute our heritage of sacred involvement in the life of a people and of persons. One of the greatest encumbrances to effective communication in the church today is the lack of knowledge of the Christian story. As we go on to investigate the role of ritual in communication, this will become more apparent. The task of encouraging individuals to anticipate manifestations of the sacred in their lives is "sore let and hindered" by this mythological illiteracy. We simply have lost the myths, the sacred stories, that in the past made us a people and sustained a contemporary sense of that deeper reality within "things." Unfortunately, we compound the problem by acting as if it did not exist. We try to communicate the faith as if a basic knowledge of the story were there. As my friend Herbert O'Driscoll remarked in a conversation, "We proceed to construct a high rise from the fourth floor up, presuming someone else has already laid the foundation and built the first three floors — and they haven't — and the whole structure collapses."

Tell the story. Oh, how we need to tell the stories, in all their power and graphic detail. Thomas Driver in *Patterns of Grace* says, "A number of theologians recently have become interested in the importance of stories. They sense that all our logical, scientific, and theological discourse is secondary. I share this belief. I have long thought that theology is to religious narrative as literary criticism is to literature — commentary upon a more basic form of expression. . . . theology has, in the course of time, removed itself too far from its roots in narrative. I find myself not only agreeing that theology originates in stories (and should tell itself more of them), but also thinking that all knowledge comes from a mode of understanding that is dramatic. Far from merely illustrating truths we already know some other way, the dramatic imagination is the means whereby we get started in any knowledge whatever.''[5]

If we do not re-immerse ourselves in the stories, we cause theology, creeds, faith, even liturgy and sacraments, to become abstract, conceptual, systematic — in other words, merely part of the pool of Cartesian data. This seems too simple to the conventional mind, addicted as it is to a steady diet of raw facts. That is because it *is* simple. The further we get behind the theology, the closer we get to personal story — the experience of God's involvement with his people. We find ourselves telling others, ''Well, this man or this woman was alone in a deserted place . . . then they saw . . . and they heard a voice . . .'' We are suddenly into very personal narrative language, the form in which the experience was first transmitted — myth, metaphor, and story. These narratives compel and challenge in a way no creed ever can, though *credo*, ''I believe,'' is the natural outcome of them. Systematic theology, necessary as it is for check and balance, simply does not have the ability to tell the story of faith. It is not of its nature to do so. As the author of the Epistle to the Hebrews so succinctly puts it, ''In many and various ways God spoke of old to our fathers . . . but in these last days he has spoken by a Son'' (1:1–2). And when that Son spoke, it was in stories and parables about doors and sheep and lost coins and patched garments and many other ingredients of the common secular life.

William J. Bausch declares, ''To the extent then, that we go back to the 'first' ways that God spoke through his prophets (in sign, symbol, metaphor and anecdote) and by his Son (in parables), to that extent we are moving into what is called narrative theology or the theology of story telling. It is going back to the original language to hear it, not as a text or as a science dissertation, but as poetry and story and all the other categories people use who strain to express the inexpressible.''[6]

But it is so difficult to restrict ourselves to telling the story. Almost irresistible is the temptation to add, when the story ends, ''Now, what the story (or the Bible) is trying to say is . . .'' Stories, particularly biblical ones, do not *try* to say anything, they *say* it. The problem is they are heard with Cartesian ears, and we are, therefore, tempted to explain meanings. Was it a whale that swallowed Jonah (the story says only "a great fish")? If so, what species? Is its throat large enough? How could a man survive inside a whale? What about digestive juices? If people need help in learning once again to tell stories, even more do they need assistance in cultivating the art of hearing in the old way. If they did, they would hear in Jonah's epic story of a God from whom you cannot run away though you flee to the ends of the earth — or into the belly of a great fish — and they would learn something of the acceptance of personal misson. They would not learn anything about ichthyology.

We have, then, two quests — to let the story tell itself, and to hear it in the old way. The way to begin is by creating opportunities and environments in which people can tell their own story and hear those of others, especially in small groups where confidence is more easily attained. One of the first things people will notice is how often they hear, "It was like . . ." With these words they are re-entering the world of metaphor and are only a few steps away from the rebirth of myth. This re-introduction to metaphor is crucial. The vast majority of Canadian adults and young people have little or no grasp of a non-literal approach to reality. They had it as a child. Our contemporary society, its values, its educational system — all contrive, as we have already noted, to idolize factual, physical data. The work of breaking through that surface reality to find the meaning that is beneath meaning, the reality that is more real than real, is going to be an uphill struggle. Conventional wisdom is a fierce opponent. However, the prize is the re-investing of sacred story with saving power, and that makes the struggle worthwhile. The more our liturgy, and especially liturgical preaching, can embody the stories of the sacred in the secular, the more we will come to expect to have something happen when we meet as community. We will look more deeply into this in the next chapter on ritual, but perhaps at this point, we could remember that the setting and context of the first eucharist was the dramatic re-telling of a story.

The total immersion in sacred story which constitutes the Passover meal for Jews is difficult for us to grasp, even when we Gentiles try to re-enact a Seder Supper. We cannot possibly feel what that ritualized, dramatized story means to the people of the Old Testament. The chilling impact of "this is my body . . . my blood . . . your new Passover lamb'' in the middle of that story is almost beyond our comprehension today. The disciples were undoubtedly thunder-struck, and their recollection of that night, after the events of the Passion and Resurrection, has given us vivid and engrossing stories of lives changed and renewed by wine made blood and bread become body.

7
New Life
for Ritual

The word *ritual* has fallen on rough times. "It's nothing but a hollow ritual" . . . "mere ritual" . . . "he's done it so often it's become a ritual." In one sense it would be so much easier if we could avoid the word, emptied as it is of its original meaning. But we cannot, for it is yet in common parlance in the church. The task is to find a way in which "hollow" ritual may be filled with new life. Long ago, rituals were powerful stuff. Fooling around with ritual could be very dangerous. Ritual was the way you came into the presence of the deity. Even more — ritual was the channel through which, in pagan belief, you assumed the deity. You would never have heard the word *mere* connected with ritual in the world of Jesus' time.

William Temple once coined a simplistic yet effective cosmological equation: God minus the world equals God; the world minus God equals nothing. Within the limitations of our finite minds it is impossible to imagine anything other than a cosmology which has God and the created world as separate entities. This is understandable, since my experience is that when I create anything it is something other than me — it is "out there," a product of my creative efforts. Be that as it may, to make sense of ritual, we must try to conceptualize a world view which accepts that the total created universe exists *within* the being of God. God is not merely the creator, he is the sustainer of creation. God's being keeps in existence all that is. Within that created and sustained order is the present world as we know it, including its past and future (see p. 79 "Sacred Time in Secular Time"). This we have called the *saeculum* — the secular world of human experience. It is interesting that we, in English, use the word *order* to describe the totality of creation. Rightly so, for the Genesis imagery powerfully describes the creative act as the Spirit of God brooding, as a mother bird on the nest, over the chaos to order it into life and light.

The destructive forces of evil within the *saeculum* strive constantly to reverse that process, to crumble the order back into chaos and to neutralize God's "Let there be light" with the power of cosmic darkness. Just as we can encounter the sacred in the secular, so in the stuff of our daily lives we may also discover the profane. Therefore a word of caution is advised. Encounters of ritual are not confined to the sacred. Deliberate, ritualized action has been part and parcel of the demonic throughout history. The Fall of Satan from heaven was preceded by "lightning war," and the German word for that is *Blitzkrieg*. The spectacles of mass conformity of the late 1930s in Hitler's Germany are grim reminders that ritual is never to be taken lightly. Truly, the glow at the end of the passageway could well be a torch in the hand of the light bearer — Lucifer!

In the ancient Babylonian rites of the New Year, a chaotic mortal conflict between the profane and the secular was enacted. Each year the profane had to be driven out so that the cosmos could be rebuilt. Then, during the ensuing year, the profane seeped back into the secular, until once again the sacred would be forced into the battle which annually insured the continuance of the secular. This primitive non-biblical myth is introduced here to illustrate the traditional nature of the sacred-profane myth and the critical place it has for aeons occupied on the stage of human history. It is by ritual that humanity has sought to encounter the sacred and to harness its power to order chaos and achieve the perceived purposes of the creator deity.

For Christians the sublime and most easily observed example of this function of ritual is in what we call "the sacraments." In baptism, for example, the profane in the life of the individual (original sin) is exorcised and the divine purpose (adoption as a child of God) for that person is achieved. This is done by means of a ritual involving the use of the secular creation (water) combined with the presence of the deity ("In the name of the Father, and of the Son, and of the Holy Spirit").

Traditionally there are four elements to ritual — symbolism, consecration, repetition, and remembrance. Symbolism can arouse an awareness of divine presence; for Christians the ultimate symbols are the bread and wine of the eucharist. Consecration enables a natural situation or material to share in a power which transcends the natural. Participants are linked to their past by repetition; this allows them to become part of the original event which they are celebrating — for example, in each eucharist the words of institution are repeated: "Our Lord Jesus Christ took bread . . ." Ritualistically the attendants at the eucharist become participants in the upper room. Remembrance is a bond pulling a community together by preserving religious tradition which is expressed in and through the ritual: remembering the great cloud of witnesses by which we are surrounded.

We have already noted that words and story are important elements of ritual. This includes both the church's story and our personal stories, both of which may embody the sacred. Ritual can and should involve movement, music, colour, aroma, light, darkness, and silence. Perhaps the most neglected element of effective ritual is silence, a particular kind of "filled" silence (we will discuss this more deeply in a moment). The careful planning, the orchestration, of all these ingredients is essential if the ritual is to "work."

What is it we are trying to achieve; how do we know if it works? If epiphany is encounter with the God who desires to be known, initiated *by* God, then ritual is nothing less than the same process from the other side, initiated by people. Ritual is an indication to God, and to ourselves, that we are serious in our intent to encounter his reality. Epiphany and ritual have the same intended end result — encounter at the deepest personal, experiential level with God. How do you know if it works? The biblical accounts are almost universal in their description of a combination of fear and delight. The presence of the revealing God always gives rise to feelings of exaltation and consternation. From Jacob's "How fearsome is this place" to Isaiah's "Woe is me, for I am undone" to John the Divine on the Island of Patmos declaring his vision of God, it is clear that effective encounters with the God who waits to reveal himself are not to be trifled with.

Let me share an experience with you. Last Easter Eve I was involved as subdeacon in a meticulously planned and imaginatively orchestrated Easter vigil. The great church was jammed, for there were to be several baptisms and a number of confirmations. That, of course, brings lots of relatives and friends, many of whom are not what one would call frequent attenders of liturgical observances. The packed nave was suddenly plunged into total darkness — nothing cuts conversation like sudden darkness in a public place. The crowded pews were instantly entombed in absolute, yet expectant silence. Then the spark of new flame flickered into life on the doorstep, and a wavering light was held on high at the tip of a tall new paschal candle. As that tiny flame battled against the enveloping darkness, a lone voice shattered the stillness with a single note, ''The light of Christ.'' The congregation's response, ''Thanks be to God,'' was almost an exhaled sigh of relief. Life and light emerging from the entombment of death and darkness.

Then tapers were held in trembling hands as that single flame passed from one to another. Gradually the solitary light became the flickering illumination of community, spreading as the resurrected life had spread — from each one's light to each neighbour's darkness. As I watched and felt what was happening I thought, ''This is really effective; here is ritual that works!'' Then we reached the chancel steps, and I turned to hold the sacred text as the deacon, by the flickering light of the paschal candle, sang the Exultet. Here now is the story — the crossing of the Red Sea, the Passover lamb, parallels in baptism, crucifixion, eucharist. Then it happened. The fidgeting started — coughs, whispers, shuffling of feet — and I suddenly realized that *they didn't know the story!* Certainly the movement, darkness, flames, silence — all the ingredients, well enacted after careful rehearsal — had worked their natural, emotional impact; but for many in that crowded nave the high rise of ritual collapsed without its underpinnings of story. I believe that what was spectacularly demonstrated that night happens in a more ordinary manner on almost every Sunday in most churches in our land. The young, the visitor, the member from another denomination, the biblically illiterate of any age — their numbers are legion — those for whom there is no story foundation for the ritual, stare blankly around in embarrassed frustration.

I did not say these were strangers to ritual; they were strangers only to *that* ritual. We are all creatures of ritual. Our society is riddled with ritual, especially rituals of passage. Marriage and death are the most ritualized events in contemporary life. I say marriage and death rather than weddings and funerals which are only the public ceremonies. The whole passage from the single to the married state and from life to death is surrounded not just with customs but with ritual. Watch the way people stand and move in a funeral parlour. It is totally unnatural; it is ritualized dance. The words spoken are almost versicle and response. The dress, the music, the flowers, the appropriate moments of charged silence — all are the ingredients of genuine ritual. Behaviour, dress, and procedures associated with marriage are even more ritualized, especially within ethnic contexts. "Bridal books" can be published with detailed directives far more rubrically demanding than any missal or *Book of Common Prayer*.

People speak of their morning ritual of shower, coffee, and whatever. This is a rite of passage — a little resurrection — from a world of dream and rest to one of wakefulness and activity. Disruption of the routine of that ritual has its effect on us. Listen to the way we speak of it: "I can't get going until I've . . ."; "I'm no good until after my first . . . in the morning."

Rituals are an essential part of our humanity, from hugs to handshakes, from bathing to bedtime stories. The symbolism, consecration, repetition, and remembrance of rituals permeate the *saeculum* of human life like the leaven that lightens the loaf of daily bread. Therefore, the rituals of divine encounter must be taken very seriously. Unlike epiphanies, they do not just happen. Because we initiate them, we must put a great deal of effort into their accomplishment. At this stage in human history the major component of that effort must be in achieving knowledge (in the biblical sense of total involvement) of the story which lies at the heart of God's intercourse with his people.

Because most church systems depend on people participation in order to exist, we feel a compulsion to involve as many as possible during the one time we are most public, the service of worship on Sunday morning. The thought of excluding anyone is repulsive. We may go to immeasurable effort to make strangers welcome and to attract the unchurched to this sacred hour on Sunday. We try very hard to make what we do attractive to all. The victim of this is ritual. That attitude was anathema to the early church. The *missa catechumenorum* — the mass of those learning the faith — was a rigidly distinct enterprise from the *missa fidelium* — the mass of the faithful. The parallel of restricting the Greek mysteries solely to the initiated was no problem to early Christians. They knew that only those who had grasped, and been grasped by, the sacred story could fully participate in the divine encounter. To allow the uninitiated in was dangerous. It meant at least confusion and at worst total failure of the ritual for all.

Something of that insight must be recaptured in contemporary ritual. First we must accept that this is no value judgement on the uninitiated. They are no less persons of worth. In fact, it is a recognition of their worth to acknowledge that their full participation in redemptive ritual demands that they be given the means of knowledgeable participation. How we go about the mechanics of this will obviously vary from situation to situation. Physical exclusion and the barring of doors, as in the early church, is blatantly inappropriate in our time. Some means of enhancing what we usually call "the ministry of the word" in sacramental acts is a first step. This includes preparation of godparents, parents, children, and the parish community for baptism; wedding preparation; education for first communion; confirmation instruction; training and rehearsal of servers, readers, and lay assistants. Much of this goes on now. All of it must be done better. The role and practice of liturgical preaching, opportunities for personal story telling apart from liturgy, Bible study — the breathing of new life into ritual is far more than merely adding banners, tapers, and eucharistic vestments to appease visual appetites.

Ritual has been described as "daughter of the dance." We are wooden in church. We presume dancing is out of place other than in avant-garde liturgical performances. But the choir, offertory, and Gospel processions, even the movement (with or without verger) of the preacher to the pulpit, are more than getting from one place to another. They have significance if only we could *see* it. Space, and where we place ourselves in it, is significant. How and when we move is significant. Posture, physical environment, music, language — nothing is mere decoration; nothing is just one-dimensional. Nothing should ever be accidental. All must be deliberate, planned, thought out carefully if ritual is to allow the sacred to shine in this, our all so immediate, *saeculum*.

We need to give more consideration to the *missa fidelium* and the thought that only the initiated, those who have knowledge of the story, may participate in the ritual. This sounds so elitist in our egalitarian times that it is difficult for us to take seriously or consider as a viable option. But leave aside the practical difficulties for a moment, and try to give some thought to these questions. Does the mere fact of gathering a group of people together create a community? Does taking, blessing, and breaking bread and taking and blessing wine in the midst of that group of people make them a eucharistic community?

I think most of us would answer No to both these questions. Surely eucharist grows out of conscious, deliberate action of community, not the other way round. Of course, the presence we seek and will find in this redemptive ritual will renew and reform our common union with each other by bringing us into common union with that which makes us holy as we can never make ourselves holy. This is precisely the point! The open invitation to those who come for any other reason than that dangerously delightful encounter is suspect.

As we stand in warm and genuine welcome of the renewed emphasis on sacramental community in the life of the church, particularly in relation to eucharist and baptism, can we give similar attention to the equally strong, equally ancient tradition, in both Catholic West and Orthodox East, of the restriction of the mysteries to those prepared to participate? We would do well to consider the significance of the retention of that tradition in the Orthodox East and of its disappearance from the seventeenth century on in the West. The date of that disappearance is not coincidental, I believe. It corresponds with the industrialization of the West, the rise of scientism, and the cult of the individual. We are told that prior to the seventeenth century, Archbishop Cranmer meant quite literally his invitatory declaration in the English "Draw near with faith," and fully intended that some would, and others would not, remain. Could our reluctance to reinstate this practice be one more facet of our Cartesian heritage, and one more reason for the stagnation of ritual in our time?

Why this emphasis on trying to reclaim and revitalize ritual? It smacks almost of a cry for a return to a medieval, magical, other worldly Christianity, and that is in absolute opposition to all we have said about incarnational communication, seeking the sacred in the nitty-gritty of our secularity. To think that is to misunder-

stand the nature of ritual and to confuse it with the esoteric
shadows of Greek mystery religions. Ritual is nothing more, and
nothing less, than a condensed version of what those who enact
it presume is going on all the time in the *saeculum*. It is a sharp
focusing, a microcosm of life itself. What we are enacting is
happening continuously, we believe, in the created order — God
intersecting human history constantly, so that history may continue. Ritual allows that intersection to be visible and open to
entry by the participants. A ritual is not a vision; it is an encounter.
It is like a passageway because it allows for two way traffic. It
permits the encounter, and provides the way back. Rituals are
necessary to allow us to assume our rightful place in relation to
the sacred, to protect us from the sacred and it from us. ''Close
encounters'' but not identity. We do not become divine; we encounter divinity.

8
Butterflies
Are Free

Epiphany and ritual — two avenues to divine encounter within the secular, two modes of what we have chosen to call incarnational communication. But to what end? Is a result intended? To describe what our expectation might be, we turn again to a scriptural image. Once more it is a name given to a specific event celebrated annually in the liturgical calendar, but used also as a verb in both scripture and literature. "Jesus took Peter, James, and John with him and led them up to a high mountain where they were alone; and in their presence he was transfigured" (Mark 9:2).

Here, strange as it may seem, is the goal of epiphany and ritual — transfiguration. "They saw Elijah appear, and Moses with him, and there they were, conversing with Jesus . . . Then a cloud appeared . . . and out of the cloud came a voice: 'This is my Son, my Beloved; listen to him'" (Mark 9:4–7).

The participants in this epiphany, Peter, James, and John, were devout Jews who, regardless of formal education, would be steeped in the tradition of their faith and culture. Judaism is not so much a creed as a way of life. Day in and day out, Sabbath after Sabbath, the history of their people, which was also their sacred story, was read and heard, repeated and responded to. Moses and Elijah therefore would be for Peter, James, and John not mere historic personages. Moses is God's Law, Elijah is the Prophets. So, the appearance of Moses and Elijah in easy conversation with Jesus presents a startling juxtaposition of the secular to the sacred. The person who had become a familiar part of their daily lives, their *saeculum*, was united with all that they knew of God's nature, will, and law. Everything that had gone before in the Law and the Prophets was symbolized for them in this "communication" with him they had come to know as teacher and friend. Then came a voice from the cloud, and for Israel from earliest times in wilderness and on Sinai, cloud was the harbinger of Jehovah. In essence the voice said, "All you have known of me in the past was in Law and Prophet. Now, in your present time, listen to this, my Beloved. He is of my very being, my Son!"

To understand the potential of this term *transfiguration,* we must grasp one critical concept. On the mountain top Jesus did not *become* the beloved Son. Transfiguration does not effect a change in nature. Jesus was revealed *as he truly was;* his essential being was disclosed. The disciples were now able to know him as beloved Son, clearly, no longer "as in a glass, darkly." What they had perhaps suspected — all the little bits and pieces of conjecture and wondering — coalesced, fell into place, and "he was transfigured in their sight." The Greek word *metamorphothe* means in English "transfigure," but we transliterate it directly as "metamorphosis." A squat, ugly, horned, green worm crawls along a tree branch, finds a likely spot, and spins a cocoon. Sometime later the little tomb cracks open and shimmering wings furtively emerge, stretch, and dry. Soon, floating free on the summer breeze, is the startlingly fragile beauty of a butterfly. The form and freedom of the butterfly were always potential but captive within the caterpillar. What had to happen was metamorphosis, transfiguration, of hidden form into the visible being.

The word *metamorphothe* is used in only two other places in the New Testament. St Paul in a most illuminating application of the verb says, "We all, with unveiled face, beholding the glory of the Lord, are being changed [transfigured], into his likeness from one degree to another"(2 Cor 3:18). There is much here to note. The action of transfiguration appears as an unveiling, a disclosure of something already there. The discovery comes about from "beholding the glory of the Lord" — what we have described as either epiphany or ritual. Also, transfiguration seems to be a gradual process, a becoming "from one degree to another," rather than a sudden conversion from one nature or being to another.

In another of his letters to the first generation of those struggling with the new life, Paul urges, "Do not be conformed to this world [*saeculum*], but be transformed [transfigured] by the renewal of your mind." The *saeculum* is not all there is. While you are in it, maintain the process of renewal, of becoming.

We are told that St Augustine offered the same advice in seemingly contradictory language, to those he baptised: ''Go . . . and become what you are.'' Transfiguration, then, is a process of manifesting your potential as a child of God. You do not have to work to become a child of God; that is a realized fact. Transfiguration is the revealing of what you are.

Many other references in the New Testament convey this concept in a variety of ways without using the actual word. Several of Jesus' strong images of the already realized but not manifested kingdom share a transfigurational sense.

> I vest in you the kingship which my Father vested in me. (Luke 22:29)
> The kingdom of God has already come among you. (Matt 12:28)
> The time has come, the kingdom of God is upon you. (Mark 1:15)
> . . . no saying, ''Look, here it is!'' or ''There it is!''; in fact, the kingdom of God is among you. (Luke 17:21)
> The kingdom of God is like yeast . . . mixed with half a hundredweight of flour till it was all leavened. (Luke 13:21)

There are many such images of the presence of God incarnated in our secular lives, waiting to be transfigured into conscious reality, hidden to be disclosed. In a variety of ways St Paul often speaks of how we must realize the reality of the transformation which has already been accomplished in us. ''If any one is in Christ, he *is* a new creation'' (2 Cor 5:17).

In this light, then, we return to our question of the role of epiphany and ritual encounters. They are not ends in themselves; they contribute to the process we call transfiguration. If they are looked upon as the totality of the process, they stagnate and die. They are enablers of action, not the action itself. The temptation to make epiphany and ritual into something permanent, something which may be grasped and contained, is all too attractive.

Again there is insight from the account of the original transfiguration epiphany. When the glorious vision fades, Peter's immediate reaction is, "Lord, let's make three tabernacles here — one for you, one for Moses, and one for Elijah." That is, "Let's enshrine our experience, hold on to it, put it in a glass case so that we can come here from time to time and revel in its glory." Christ's answer is, "Back down the mountain, boys. The world awaits." Back to the ever-present *saeculum.* "Take your epiphany where it belongs; use it to enlighten the process of being what I have already made you — those called and sent, disciples and apostles." Down the mountain they trudge to find themselves confronted by the critical immediacy of mission. An epileptic child, whose illness had defied the healing attempts of the other disciples, lies waiting. Epiphanies are given to be embodied in the realities of daily human existence.

Encounters with the sacred contribute to our self-realization. They point the direction as we "wander dazed in the abundant universe," to use Whitehead's phrase. Traditional theology refers to "fallen humanity," "sin," or even "original sin." Modern psychology and psycho-theology speak of our "estrangement" from our true selves, from other persons, and from God. Regardless of the terminology we choose to describe it, the point is that our view of ourselves and our relationship with others and with God is myopic — quite literally "out of focus." Transfiguration is the process of discovery of the truth about ourselves and where we stand in relation to the world. *Discover* is exactly the correct verb, for that process is literally taking off the cover, exposing something already there to the light of self-knowledge and to the knowledge of the reality of the sacred.

These deeper insights are not mere confirmations of what we already knew. And they are not new data to assist us in managing a world which is "out there" — external to us. Transfigurational insights transform the world which includes us. What is changed is our way of dwelling in the world. The process of transfiguration affects our mode of being. It causes us to imagine what we might be or do. It gives us the opportunity to envision possibilities for an authentic human existence in which we would no longer be separated from each other, the world, or God. It means an end to estrangement, the forgiving of sin, the renewing of humanity, "the changing into his likeness from one degree to another."

Transfiguration might be compared to looking at a familiar scene, or the face of a much loved person, through the view finder of a camera, and then adjusting the focus, bringing the subject into a new sharpness of detail within the context of a larger picture. This is seeing the familiar scene or face in a new way. It affirms the familiar, what we already have information about, but shifts the focus so that we relate to it — we know it —in a more abundant fashion. This enriches the environment of our living.

In no way do I mean to suggest that this process is confined to epiphanies and rituals. They are high points, pinnacles of perception, beacons on the journey, to be sure, but they are not the journey. Transfiguration happens in personal relationships in a variety of ways. Sometimes love is confirmed and strengthened by a physical act, yet at other times simply by a look or a word which says profoundly, "I understand." It can happen, as well, when an experience of absolute beauty and oneness with the physical environment deepens our cosmology and allows us to share the creator's declaration, "It is good!"

There is a second dynamic to transfiguration which is much more radical. It involves turning that which is familiar upside down or inside out. It radically transforms the norms of our perception of the world and ourselves. It calls into question the manner in which we exist, yet affirms who we are in spite of what we are. Radical as that sounds, it is the view of a world we find in the New Testament. This is the place where the last are first, the meek inherit, and the rich are paupers. Here is the ground where God is present *and* transcendant, where the kingdom is within you and still to come. This is where to live you must die, and where the master is the servant of all. Children have no difficulty at all with this kind of world. Fairy tales and many classical myths are set in it. Perhaps this is why Jesus said that unless we become child-like, our hope for life in the kingdom is slim indeed.

The remarkable thing about this dimension of transfiguration that radically calls into question the reality of the world as we normally see it, is that we are attracted to it as moths to a flame. We want it to be the true picture of reality. It feels right! Yet we are terrified of its implications. We are drawn and repelled at the same time because its source is God. Because we are created to relate to him, we are pulled by the cords of divine love, yet we are reluctant to draw near. We do not want to get too close, for we know it means the death of much we hold dear. Transfigured reality allows me to see things as they are and as they might be simultaneously, to look at myself in the world and envision my new self in a new world. This is inspiring and fearful at once. We ourselves experience something of the awesome attractiveness we have observed in many of the Old Testament epiphanies.

The significance of another scriptural insight into transfigured reality may only now, in this era of technological wonder, be evident. In the letter to the Romans, St Paul makes a statement of tremendous importance to our consideration of the transfiguration of the *saeculum*. ''The created universe waits with eager expectation for God's sons to be revealed . . . Up to the present, we know, the whole created universe groans in all its parts as if in the pangs of childbirth. Not only so, but even we, to whom the Spirit is given as first fruits of the harvest to come, are groaning inwardly while we wait for God to make us his sons, and set our whole body free'' (Rom 8:19–23). I would not try to claim that St Paul had in mind what I see in this passage. The cosmology of his time, a seven storied universe and flat earth, could not have anticipated transplanting human organs, test-tube life, space travel, electronic satellite communication, and all the other technological advances by which we exercise more and more control over our environment. Yet those of us who believe in the transforming power of God's Spirit can see in these wonders the ''harvest to come'' which is the result of our knowing and understanding God and his creation. The more our *saeculum*, part of ''the whole created universe,''is transfigured, the more it becomes what it is already — the cosmos upon which God looked and smiled and said, ''It is very good.''

I am not entirely naive. The very advances I have listed, and thousands of others which could be added, might just as easily spell the end, rather than fulfilment, of our *saeculum*. That is the risk God took when he first created us free to love. It is the same risk he dares whenever he assists us to transfigure any part of his created order. Our chaos can apparently consume his order any time we choose. Perhaps it is only through transfiguration that we have any hope at all. In a knowing relationship with the creator lies the possibility to realize our potential and the potential of our universe. Our own transfiguration is in a mysterious way involved with that of the created order, for we are one with it. The cataclysmic danger lies in our forgetting this awesome fact. We destroy the world every time we consider ourselves external to it and able to use it for our own ends. This fact, I am sure, lies at the heart of St Paul's words to the Romans. We will not be transformed apart from the transformation of the cosmos which includes us.

We do not usually think of our spiritual journey in terms of transfiguration, and it is not a simple thing to grasp. But we need to keep it as the goal of epiphany and ritual. It is also the goal of incarnational communication — assisting the people of God to realize all their potential, truly to become what they are. That is indeed a glorious thing when it happens.

9
Of Signs
and Symbols,
Images and Myth

There is much confusion around our common use of the words
image, sign, and *symbol.* Imagery and symbolism seem to be virtually interchangeable terms in common usage. There are,
however, important distinctions between them, and between
either of them and *sign.* At a relatively superficial level the dif-
ferences are quite simple. A sign is a directional pointer which
makes an unknown reality known — for example, "Danger Thin
Ice," red means "Stop." We say that red signifies (that is, it sign-
ifies) "Stop." An image is a particular type of sign. In a sense,
it is a pointer also, in that it indicates a reality other than itself.
However, an image aims at reproducing as accurately as possible the reality to which it points. So we declare a marble bust
or oil portrait or photograph to be an image of a person, or refer
to a child as the "spitting image" of his grandfather.

A symbol is something of a quite different order. The Greek
word was *sum-ballein* which meant literally "to throw together."
It referred in ancient times to a tally or mark of some sort used
as a means of verification or identification. One common way to
produce a *sum-ballo* was to take a piece of pottery and break it
in an irregular manner. I take one piece with me and, on my
return, my piece must match yours to verify that I am who I say
I am. There is, then, even in the original usage, a sense of authenticity without identification; the broken pottery shard is not me,
yet it identifies me. There is in symbol a power and depth which
enables it not so much to represent reality as to disclose it by making it present. In this special way symbols participate in that which
they make present. From its original meaning, symbol carries the
force of breaking and separating in order to reunite and verify.
A symbol is something that points to a reality while uniting us
with it, bringing us and it together, relating us. I suppose the
supreme example for Christians is a cross, or the making of the

sign of the cross on oneself. This is a sign and an image, but it goes beyond them and "throws us together" with reality in the manner of a symbol.

So what? Does it really matter whether we call a cross a sign, an image, or a symbol? I believe it matters a great deal if we are sincere in our attempts to communicate more effectively. It matters because, if you are not totally sure of what you are using when you set out to represent reality, you will fail. It is as simple as that. Images do not do what symbols do, and signs are seldom adequate for anything other than information. Each has a role in our communication package, but if we confuse those roles we stand much less chance of successful understanding.

Let us go back and delve a little deeper into the capabilities and limitations of these three communication tools.

We have observed that red is an accepted sign for "Stop" or "Danger." That is a totally arbitrary decision. There is no inner necessity for red to mean stop; it could as easily have been agreed in time past that green would indicate stop. In the Orient the colour of mourning is white, the direct opposite of our practice in the West. This points up one of the serious limitations of signs; they require a degree of common or conventional "language." Illiteracy can be fatal when approaching a sign which says, "Danger, High Voltage." Likewise, the meaning of much imagery is missed if observors do not know in whose image the statue, painting, or photo is made. It may be a perfect likeness, but if I do not know of whom, it is a useless communication tool.

There is another class of sign which has a different relationship to the reality to which it points. Here the relationship arises from nature. The best example is smoke signifying fire. From experience we have learned to associate one with the other, so that there is even a common saying: "Where there's smoke there's fire." Smoke is a sign of fire, it is not an image of it. If we are walking up a hill and see smoke on the other side of the crest, we presume there is something on fire over there, yet we have not yet seen flames. The fact that the Israelites in the wilderness regarded pillars of smoke or mountains shrouded in smoke as symbols not of fire but of the presence of God, shows that even a sign so universally accepted can have a symbolic power added to it. For the Israelites smoke was not merely a sign of God; it certainly was not an image of God. It was a means of identifying, authenticating, and expressing an *experience* of the presence of God.

It may have seemed strange that, thus far in such a detailed investigation of modes of communication of the sacred, I have said little, if anything, of myth. This has been deliberate. There was a time when I would have described much of what I have called epiphany as myth. I would have designated myth as one of the chief tools of ritual. Today I hesitate to do so. The word *myth* has been robbed of its true meaning. The word has not ceased to be used; would that it had! It has, rather, become very much common parlance and (I shudder) a frequently employed tool of the advertising and headline copy writer. Now, to our chagrin, myth assaults us from commercials daily, as in "Dispel the myth that detergent cannot remove ugly grass stains from your children's jeans." The word has become synonymous with "a long-held untruth." "That's only a myth" trips easily from the tongue of young and old alike as the quickest way to discredit another's pronouncement.

Seldom do I admit defeat in the battle for the niceties of linguistic proprieties. This time I do! So common is the use of *myth* as a synonym for *false*, that no amount of explaining that myth actually connotes something truer than true, more real than reality, will suffice. Besides, if one must take time to explain how one is using, or not using, a term on each occasion, then the term has ceased to be useful. I deeply regret this. When one observes the depth of spiritual verity a C.S. Lewis or a J.R.R. Tolkien can achieve through the deliberate, inspired creation of modern myth, it is a shame to have to abandon the name of their genre. Most regrettable of all is to be sorely misunderstood when one calls a classic of our spiritual heritage a myth. Or worse, when one refers to a portion of scripture as mythical, to have the immediate response, "Oh, you don't believe the Bible! You say parts of it aren't true." I have just paid scripture the ultimate compliment of being a channel of communication of the divine in a way no supposedly "true" history book could ever be, and the reaction is that I think scripture is not to be trusted! Having fought the good fight for too long, I rest from my labours, at least from those that have proven useless. In this book I set out to find ways of speaking about what I used to call myth which might convey at least some of that magnificent concept. I sought terminology which, although it might require explanation when first used, would arrive on the scene with no "baggage" to be unloaded.

We are about to consider metaphor. With it I walk a very fine edge. The term itself has not had wide enough regular use to pose a problem, but the concept will take some effort for our conventional Cartesian minds to grasp. As my mentor at the College of Preachers, Dr Taylor Scott, said to me in his usual graphic southern manner, "When you're talkin' metaphor, you're paddlin' against the stream." I am still convinced, however, that it can be a useful verbal instrument. In fact, I believe that metaphor is the best communication tool available to us for expressing human experience of the sacred in the secular. It is the language of epiphany, ritual, and transfiguration, whether that language be spoken, written, sung, danced, played, or painted. We will need all the metaphors we can create to build the new speech we seek.

10
The Tension Space
of Metaphor

To speak of love or communicate with children is to use metaphor.
To express your feelings or describe any experience of the sacred
in your life is to use metaphor. The language of transfiguration,
epiphany, and ritual is metaphor. The mode of incarnational communication is metaphor. As we have already noted, if you give
people the opportunity to share sacred story or their own stories,
within minutes they will be saying, "Well, it was like . . ." and
will have entered the world of metaphor. People who would
strenuously declare that they cannot understand poetry, who
would be hard pressed even to define metaphor, will soon
discover they live in a world shot through with it. Human intercourse is impossible without it. The sad thing is that we utilize,
consciously, so little of its potential.

The Greek word *metaphora* literally means a transfer of
something from one person, or place, to another — to "carry
over" a space. So, in a literary sense, it has come to mean the
transfer of meaning from one thing to another. The classic definition in grammar and rhetoric is "a special kind of figure of speech
which states an identity between two entities that cannot literally be equated." An often quoted example is Robbie Burns's
famous, "O, my luv is like a red, red rose." His beloved and the
rose cannot be equated. No one would presume he meant she
was identical to a rose, with prickly thorns growing from green
limbs. The delicate symmetry and fragrance of the flower are
transferred to her by metaphor, but she and the rose are not the
same. The equation is the diametric opposite of the metaphor.
Equal signs destroy metaphors. Burns could not have said, "O,
my luv *is* a red rose," unless he preferred horticulture to
humanity. Within metaphor there must be space to maintain the
individuality of each element and to build a bridge of significance
between them. This is why our Cartesian minds have difficulty
with metaphor. We want to insert equal signs in all our
communications.

"What does it mean?" is the equal sign we want to interpose in the space of metaphor. If it *means*, it can be described literally, it is information about something. Metaphor is not the language of meaning; it is the expression of experience, the stuff of story. The truth of metaphor can never be fully explained; there is always something left over when the explanation is done. Similarly, religion is the realm of reality that can never be literally described. That is why metaphors root or ground every major religious tradition in human history. The power of metaphor is in its linking the "here" with the "not here,"the "now" with the "then" (past or future). That is why we could, in the last chapter, call it the language of the world of radical transfiguration. Metaphor builds a suspension bridge between the world I inhabit and the world that Rudolph Otto calls "the numinous," the "wholly Other." The two worlds, sacred and secular, are not identical. The space of metaphor protects us from the blasphemy of pretending the secular can be sacred. Metaphor allows us to bridge from one to the other, allows the transcendant to be linked to the immanent, the kingdom to be within and not yet.

This raises the question of the relationship of theology to metaphor. In one sense, theology is all metaphor, for obviously we cannot speak of God literally. Faith statements (the essence of theology) are attempts to explain the experience of God's people. But when all the explanations are done, there always seems to be something left over. That "something left" is the mother of metaphor. Although creeds attempt to explain how people have experienced God's actions on the stage of human history, they lack the flames of the burning bush and the blinding light of the Damascus road. To regard the Nicene Creed as a metaphor rather than a definitive list of data would, for many, enhance its creed-ability. Explanation and metaphor are married in the communication of religious experience.

Before we proceed any further, let me correct an impression that may have been given so far. Metaphor is by no means limited to figures of speech. Our world of metaphor must expand beyond spoken and written communication. One of the reasons the church today fails so often to incarnate communication, and therefore communicates so poorly, is its insistence on limiting metaphor to speech and, for the most part, written or printed speech in the bargain. We would do well to look in the rear-view mirror to see how those who came before us once relied on the metaphors of stained glass and architecture, dance and drama, changing seasons and sacred story to embody their communication with a people who read no print but understood (knew) language of all-at-once sensual immediacy. If we can say that metaphor has grounded all forms of religion, we can also declare that poetry, ritual, music, drama, story-telling, painting, and sculpture have always been the primary languages of religious expression.

Metaphor is always in process. It gives me the feeling of being somehow drawn in. It invites me to make of it what I bring to it. How I experience a metaphor (I refuse to use the phrase ''what a metaphor means to me'') may not be how you experience the same metaphor. You may not see a metaphor that I see. You may hurry by the crimson flowered bush while I'm frantically tearing off my shoes. This does not necessarily imply that I will be able to say what an effective metaphor does to me. The full experience of a metaphor is felt, not always conceptualized. It is not of the world that can be measured and reported. Its significance is discovered in participation. It derives content from my experience of my whole self in relation to something other than my self. That is one of the reasons why a heavily systematized church fears metaphor. Metaphor is intellectually uncontrollable. Metaphors will not fit into catechisms to be memorized by rote by ecclesiastical clones. Metaphor is the language of very individualized experience. That is its power, its glory, and its short-coming for the literal mind. That is, however, what could make it the salvation of lively faith in the church today. Liturgy, ritual, sacraments, parish life and programs are all in place as vessels waiting to be filled to the brim with living metaphors. (We must take some time, in a moment, to examine what we might do to find these metaphors of life, but first let us be sure that we understand just what goes on inside the metaphor, what gives it power.)

There is a tension in the space within a metaphor. This tension draws and repels, joins and keeps separate. There are architectural structures which physically illustrate the nature of such tension. The suspension bridge is one. The structure of the bridge wants to collapse, to fall down. In doing so, pressure is exerted on the ends of the bridge to push back into the sides of the chasm over which the bridge extends. As long as those ends remain anchored, one force will push against the other to maintain the tension and suspend the structure over the space.

The other example is even more spectacular. The flying buttress made the soaring triumph of the Gothic arch possible. The awesome interior spaces of the Gothic cathedrals of the world are unencumbered with supporting pillars because of the space maintained by tension within the flying buttresses. The huge, heavy vaulted roof exerts massive pressure down, forcing the ends of the supporting arches out, desperately trying to push the walls outwards. Outside the walls the flying buttresses arch over to the top of the straining walls. They exert pressure in attempting to collapse in the opposite direction. The balancing forces result in the glory of the Gothic. Incidentally, this construction also allows the walls to be ''weakened'' by vast ''holes'' which bathe the interior with the flaming visual metaphors of stained glass. Without the flying buttresses, thick masonry walls would entomb the nave in perpetual gloom.

The first time I can recall consciously experiencing the tension space of metaphor physically expressed was several years ago in Coventry. Since I first saw it in the illustrated account of the rebuilding of the war-devastated cathedral, Epstein's sculpture of Michael the archangel vanquishing Satan, *A Phoenix at Coventry*, had haunted me.[7] I had never been so captured by a photographic image of a work of art. It spoke to me of a power I could not define. I dearly longed to see the sculpture hanging on the resurrected cathedral's entrance wall. I wanted to touch it, stare at it from every available angle, experience it, and discover wherein lay the power. Finally, during a brief visit, the moment came. My family gave up on me and, after some minutes moved on. But I could not. The sculpture was even more than I had imagined, yet still the secret eluded me until I began to photograph it.

Then, there it was! Through the viewfinder of my camera it suddenly came into focus. As I looked the length of Satan, from his feet to his head, I saw the small space between the outstretched great toe of Michael's left foot and the forehead of Satan. The entire power of the piece is concentrated in the tension of that tiny space. Satan is literally cross-eyed staring at that toe. He knows that if it moves and touches him he is doomed. The whole metaphoric struggle between good and evil in the *saeculum* is compressed into that minuscule chasm. It can neither widen nor close! I was reminded of another great tension space, a space of creativity, between God's outstretched finger and that of Adam, stretching across the ceiling of the Sistine Chapel in Rome (that one I have yet to see, other than in pictures).

I learned two valuable lessons forcefully that day. I realized that the physical world abounds in metaphor, not only in the verbal constructs of humankind. I also saw, as I had never seen before, a physical expression of the space which must be maintained if metaphor is to work. I felt the tension which inhabits that space. Realizing, seeing, feeling — such knowledge is lost in the world of information. Nothing of what happened to me that day could have been experienced from the most detailed description of that sculpture, every bit of data available on it, or even its representation in a photograph. *Encounter* — that's the magic word!

Contemplating the relationship of the two sides of that space in Epstein's work revealed something else. We are so accustomed to equating the words *Satan* and *devil* that we forget something. That is not angel staring down at devil; it is angel staring at angel. Lucifer, ancient Hebrew tradition tells us, was for a time God's favourite. He was the light-bearer throughout the cosmos. But he pushed that position of prestige too far, presumed too much, and fell like a blazing star — not to hell but to earth, into the *saeculum!*

And so what we see frozen in bronze on the wall of coventry is a classic example of what happens when a metaphor is pushed too far. It "rolls over" into the negative image of itself. For example, if parental love — a source of nurture, enabling, growth, and protection — is pushed too far, it reverses into a smothering embrace of psychological, if not physical, death. The negative mirror image of parental love is child abuse. If patriotism, love of and devotion to one's country, is pushed too far, it flips into totalitarianism, the master race, and *Mein Kampf.* Then Lucifer's *Blitzkrieg* flames on earth as it did in heaven. If orthodoxy and unswerving service to the church are on one side of the tension space, the flames of the inquisitor's stake are on the other. The space must be maintained, the tension cannot be released, neither Satan nor Michael dares to move.

All of this is vital to our consideration of how we can reclaim the kind of communication that enacts what it intends to accomplish. Metaphor is the operative medium of incarnational, or sacramental, communication. Through it we may encounter the sacred in our *saeculum* without being absorbed. I remain "I," God remains "God," but the metaphor which bridges the space of the encounter enables me to become what I am and to carry out the *mysterion* — the "secret" plans revealed to me. I would not mean to push this to the point of proving anything, but I find it interesting that there is also a space, an anatomical space, at the physical base of human communication. The impulses that travel through the human nervous system and make it possible for us to think, act, or move as human beings must jump a minute space called a synapse at the point of junction between one nerve cell and the next. If that space of one ten-thousandth of a millimetre were closed, the transmission of the impulses that allows communication with our environment would cease. A physical space which must be bridged, a microcosm of metaphor, is all that keeps us from silence and death.

Although "my luv is like a red, red rose" is a typical metaphor, the space does not always require "like." Sometimes we can say "is" and yet maintain the metaphor. This can bring to our communication a "freeze-frame" quality of startling effectiveness. The immediacy of this sort of metaphor is also its danger. Literal minded audiences may miss the subtlety. The risk is a calculated one, however, for such vivid images may achieve even more effective communication, at a much deeper level, than the more superficial "this is like that." Shakespeare's "All the world's a stage" is not an equation; it is a metaphor. We have no illusions that the bard equated his cosmos to a platform of boards. Yet, in day to day living, the truth of that metaphor is more and more evident through observation of human behaviour. The metaphor was one of Jesus' favourite tools for arresting and shattering the dead, conventional religiosity of individuals. To the crowds he told parables: "The kingdom of heaven is like . . ." But to the individual seeker of truth, the response was the metaphor of immediacy.

Nicodemus approaches, warily, after darkness has fallen, looking furtively over his shoulder to make certain no other members of the religious establishment will see him in conversation with this radical new teacher. The risk to his reputation certainly gives evidence of his sincerity, as does his opening greeting: "Rabbi, we know that you are a teacher sent from God; no one could perform these signs of yours unless God were with him"(John 3:1–2). He pauses, waits politely, expectantly, for the profound spiritual truth which he has come to find. Jesus looks intently at him and replies, "You have to be born over again." You can almost see Nicodemus shaking his head, "How's that again? The size of me now, entering my mother's womb a second time? You are kidding, aren't you? Perhaps you didn't understand the question."

Jesus tries again. The spiritual life is like the wind. You can feel it, hear it, experience its effect on you; but you cannot see it. You know neither where it started nor where it will end up. How can a leader in spiritual things not see and understand? If he cannot see the sacred in the things of this earth, he will never unlock the door to the kingdom he seeks. We have heard these images and had them interpreted in sermons so often that Nicodemus's incredulity is difficult for us to appreciate. We must recall that Nicodemus is hearing with the ears of a rigidly trained Pharisee, through centuries of tradition, law upon law, precept upon precept.

There is no neat wrap up conclusion to this dramatic, moving vignette. If it were a TV show, it would simply "fade to black." We are left hanging and wondering, but we do find out what came of it. A short two weeks later Nicodemus raises the only voice of calm, the only cry for justice in the Sanhedrin's discussion of drastic action to silence Jesus. The change in Nicodemus, the rebirth he previously could not comprehend, came about because explanations satisfy momentarily but metaphors haunt for a lifetime.

In response to the frequent, "Who are you?" Jesus was almost annoying in his reliance on metaphor. He said that he was a door, a pathway, a light, a vine, bread, and even, "My flesh is real food; my blood is real drink." Many reacted negatively: "This is more than we can stomach! Why listen to such talk?" (John 6:60). Others could relate to this dramatic, metaphoric manner of presenting reality. Jesus' declaration to them is revealing: "Turning to the Jews who had believed him, Jesus said, 'If you dwell within the revelation I have brought, you are indeed my disciples; you shall know the truth, and the truth shall set you free' ''(John 8:31–32).

''To dwell within the revelation'' is as close a paraphrase of ''incarnating communication'' as you are likely to find in scripture. The result of that sort of relating to the incarnate word is knowing the truth, and being set free to become what you are.

The whole of St John's Gospel is a series of examples illustrating the observation made in the first chapter: ''He was in the world; but the world, though it owed its being to him, did not recognize him'' (John 1:10). In confrontation after confrontation, a seemingly endless stream of folk from every walk of life in Jewish society appear to ask some variation of, ''Who are you?'' There seems no end to the changes Jesus can ring on the metaphors of his being. Some heard, were haunted, and changed; but most cried, ''He is possessed; he is raving. Why listen to him?'' (John 10:29). Truly, ''He entered his own realm, and his own would not receive him.'' (John 1:11). The difficulty of seeing truth beneath physical ''facts'' does not appear, after all, to have been an invention of Descartes in the seventeenth century.

I mentioned earlier that we are at a disadvantage because the great stories of scripture have been interpreted and explained to us so often that they have lost most of their immediacy. Words have been worked and reworked for generations and have become multi-layered in their meaning. We need to be wary of this so that those multi-meanings become aids instead of blocks to communication. For example, *Herod* is the proper name of a specific King appearing in a biblical story. But Herod is more than that. Herod is also the slaughter of innocent babes, violent injustice in a corrupt society. *Wilderness* is more than a word in the Bible; it is a state of mind and being for individuals and for entire peoples. And so it goes with a store of such multi-faceted verbal gems — fire, cloud, Judas, Pharaoh, lamb. Will *Samaritan* ever mean someone from Samaria, or not be preceded by ''good''?

Consideration of such words must not only take account of their present meaning but also emphasize the human drama which gives them their power. It is better to point to the mountaintop experiences of modern life than to discuss whether the

Transfiguration took place on Hermon or Tabor. This is a critical point for those who wish to communicate the meaning of biblical image and story. The Exodus is about what happened to a slave people escaping from bondage. But it is more than that. It is about how I escape from slavery, how God hears my cry today and parts the terrible seas to bring me out of whatever enslaves me and makes me less than God intended me to be when he called me into being. Metaphor is the bridge between his story and my story. Its construction is not easy, even though we have material and adequate tools. No one knows that better than a Christian poet such as T.S. Eliot.

> There are hands and machines
> And clay for new brick
> And lime for new mortar
> Where the bricks are fallen
> We will build with new stone
> Where the beams are rotten
> We will build with new timbers
> Where the word is spoken
> We will build with new speech.

(from "The Rock")

11
Implications and Ingredients

Speaking Publicly and Hearing Privately

When I was a young, newly-ordained curate, I was surprised one day by my rector while we were preparing for a Boy Scout annual church parade. As usual, two young lads had been chosen by the Scout master to participate in the service. The rector had asked them to come to the church to practise their parts. He proceeded to rehearse them in the saying of several of the prayers to be used. Later I expressed some consternation at this, as I had presumed they would read lessons. The rector's response has stayed with me. "Richard, God can understand anything, the people can't!" It is difficult for us to realize the impact that reading aloud made on pre-literate people. Both in Old Testament times and in the history of the church until recently, the leaders in worship ceremoniously exposed scrolls, manuscripts, and books of holy writ before an illiterate, uneducated crowd; chanted or read a prescribed section; and then removed them from sight. It almost seemed that to leave them exposed to the view of unlettered, common folk risked contamination. There was an almost magical manipulation of the sacred presence inherent in those readings.

For St Benedict (echoing my wise rector of old) *lectio* (the act of reading) meant an activity which, like chanting and writing, requires the participation of the whole body and the whole mind. If we have difficulty accepting such a major role for reading aloud in the church of today, it is even more difficult for us to comprehend how people listened in the past. Throughout the Middle Ages reading in church was called "listening to the voices of the pages." This is what has been referred to as "acoustical reading." It sounds very McLuhanish but is nonetheless true that, since the invention of printing and the universality of literacy, people do not read this way themselves, and they do not hear or remember what is said to them without a great deal of conscious effort. That much effort is seldom forthcoming on the average Sunday morning in North America. All the more reason to heed my former rector's admonition.

In the rush to involve laity in public worship, we seem to presume that the logical place to begin is in the reading of lessons, and the more members of the congregation we can involve, the better. When I was a national church staff member and therefore a non-parochial priest, I spent most of my Sundays ''filling in'' in a variety of parishes. My observation is that little, if any, preparation is given to readers, no assessment of abilities is evident, and in the vast majority of cases the results are deplorable. Certainly there are exceptions, but one of the glaring realities of today's liturgical life is the virtual meaninglessness of the lections. Even if they can be heard physically, seldom does the story ''get off the page.'' Sometimes one receives a distinct impression that the reader has not the foggiest notion of what the passage is all about.

The answer is not to place Bibles in pews with the expectation that the congregation will follow along. That fails to recognize what is happening in the lections. The reading, if presented as it deserves to be, is an invitation to a corporate activity. It is a participatory act of reader and hearer. I am reminded of the French expression for what we, in English, so coldly call ''going to a play.'' The French say, ''J'assiste a la pièce'' — that is, ''I *assist* in the performance of the play'' — simply by being there and listening. Part of the new life for ritual lies in our recapturing a sense of expectation when someone approaches the lectern or processes down the aisle and opens the scriptures to read.

Obviously, all of this applies equally to listening to sermons, and to their preparation. Imagination is totally essential to the preacher. Most of what has been said thus far of story, transfiguration, and metaphor particularly, applies directly to the task of the preacher, especially in the context of the eucharist. The homilist must seek constantly to uncover ''unseen'' relationships between things, and metaphor is the means. Also the hearers of sermons and homilies need to do their own metaphor building. This requires conscious effort to bring their *saeculum* to the relationship, to look for bridges between the scriptures, the preaching, and their own situation. They must listen ''with their mind's eye''; and visualize the bridge between homily and life. In this sense each one will hear a different sermon. Listening to scripture or preaching in this manner requires energy. It is no coincidence, I believe, that we use an energy metaphor to denote whether a message attracts us or not. We are either "turned on" or "turned off."

Response and Participation

Some of our ability to participate in ritual is governed by our approach to its sacred space. We have been conditioned, especially in the modern West, to enter our sacred spaces with reverence, but this does not mean that our sensibilities should be suppressed in a trance-like stupor. That would be to surround worship, and the ritual space, with an enforced únnatural hush. There is no evidence of that in the church's early days. St Jerome is said to have described worship in his day as a noisy affair. He was writing around AD 400, at about the time the Te Deum was composed. He remarked that the Amen of the people "resounded like heavenly thunder." Perhaps it is our Anglo-Saxon reserve, though many of today's church members are not of that lineage and show little of that reserve outside church walls! But in mainline churches today in this country, it is difficult to obtain even a quiet, audible Amen of assent to anything spoken. Contrast that with Spanish congregations crying out Amen five times after each of the petitions of the Lord's Prayer, or Coptic Christians loudly affirming Amen after each phrase as the priest recites the consecration prayer in the eucharist, and then at its end shouting, "We believe, and testify, and give praise"!

Ritual is, by its very nature, participatory and dialogic. If ritual today is comatose, it is because we have turned it into performance for an audience rather than an event involving participants. Group hymn singing is one kind of participation. But antiphonal singing is closer to the kind of mutually responsive participation that breathes life into ritual. There are still vestiges of antiphony in the versicles and responses and the alternative verse reading of psalms, but even these seem to be out of their element in an otherwise non-participatory presentation to the congregation. Noise wakes people up and, conversely, wide awake people make noise. After all, we have been commanded to "make a joyful noise unto the Lord," and the visions of heaven in scripture consistently depict a place in which the sound of singing, and the antiphonal versicles and responses of all sorts of creatures, is never dimmed. There does not appear to be much room for contemplative silence in the courts of heaven.

This is recognition, perhaps unconscious, of a basic fact of human relationships which has been, in our time, described by the philosophical discipline called phenomenology. Making noise, calling attention to one's own existence, is interrelated with the process of going out of oneself, projecting oneself towards someone else. Relationship, in other words, requires externalizing in the noise we call speech. Aphasia, the loss of speech, is a disorder that inhibits an individual from interacting fully with anyone. In a more commonly experienced example, the best way to learn a language is to participate in a communal life — we call it "immersion." The same holds true of the language we call ritual. We have returned once more to the incarnation, the embodiment, of communication.

By making noise in ritual we do not, by any means, indicate an uncontrolled babble (Babel). There are holy and unholy noises, sacred and profane communication. The noise of ritual (and it certainly is not confined to speech) is tightly controlled and deliberately planned, as is every other element. *Orchestrated* is the best word, with all it implies of parts assigned to various members of an ensemble, with diminuendo and crescendo and, above all, an overriding harmony. In such a scenario the celebrant ceases to be a solo performer and becomes a skilled conductor. This metaphor also reminds us that at the heart of the final, resultant harmony lies rehearsal, practice, and the homework of participants in preparation for "playing their parts." No one ever said this kind of communication is easy! Effective, yes; simple, no!

Sounds of Silence

"Be still, and know that I am God." All we have said about the noisy language of ritual in no way precludes moments of intense silence. Silence, it seems, terrifies us, whether it be in conversation or in public worship. We have an absolute compulsion, it would appear, to fill all the spaces with something — anything! It has been said that Anglicans cannot even move from point A to point B without singing a hymn. We feel we must cover the silences, obliterate them. Contemporary liturgies leave more silences, usually as opportunities for those in attendance to add individual petitions in intercessions or thanksgivings. These, however, are not the intense silences of which I speak. There is one such silence specifically anticipated in the eucharist — at the fraction, the moment of breaking of the bread. This could be one of the "filled" silences of ritual if we could assist people to work with it. We need to be taught what it means to fill, to super-charge a silence so that it becomes a powerful means of communicating reality in depth. Filled silences embody reality. In the stillness, as the scripture says, you can know God.

The fraction gives opportunities for such an experience. In the eucharist we take bread and wine — manufactured products, tokens of all that we make and do and have and are — that is, symbols of our *saeculum*. We bless them in the Jewish manner by giving thanks over them. We offer bread and wine. We believe that in the act of offering eucharist (thanksgiving) God in some way takes those elements into his very being and gives them back to us — looking, tasting, smelling, weighing the same, but changed. They have become vehicles of the presence of Christ in our lives.

We said, however, that the bread and wine were symbols of all we are, all we do, all that we "make with our hands" (the literal translation of *manu-factum*). So, as we observe and participate in the ritual movement of the offertory procession, we see, carried to and placed upon the altar, "ourselves, our souls and bodies." In similar fashion, again inexplicable, we can see our lives in all their complexity — in joy and sorrow, hope and despair — taken into the very being of God, blessed, and given back now as "reasonable, holy and living sacrifice." Our life situations, as we leave the eucharist, look, feel, seem the same, but they are changed, for they are now vehicles of sacred presence.

We break the bread. Why do we break it? Not only because it is necessary to break bread to distribute it, or simply because Jesus did. We break it because the *saeculum* it symbolizes is full of brokenness, and he who commanded us to do it is also broken for us. If we would, we could fill that silence. We could hear in it all the screams and sobs and pain of our individual and corporate brokenness. We could see all the headlines and TV news clips, the faces of all our broken relationships. And with the "crack," the fracture of Christ's body, we would know healing. That breaking embodies our brokenness, since "the chastisement he bore is health for us and by his scourging we are healed" (Is 53:5).

This kind of silence is the exact opposite of our common phrase, "a dead silence." This is charged with life. We usually think of silence in an auditory sense; it has to do with the absence of sound. But when we talk about a filled silence, the descriptions strangely tend to become visual. We speak of focusing, seeing in the silence, envisioning. When I work to achieve this kind of stillness, I try to see in my mind's eye what or whom it is with which I want to fill it. It may be faces or situations or descriptions I have heard or read about but never seen. For me it is a time of extreme effort to concentrate, to focus very deliberately. It is the direct opposite of what has often been expected — "shutting out" the world. That would be the silence of emptying one's thoughts; this is the silence of totally concentrated thought. The practice of such focusing is not easy. "Seeing" our lives placed on the altar during the offertory and "seeing" all the brokenness in our experience in the silence before the fraction are not going to happen involuntarily or without strenuous effort. However, this action of focused intensity is a means whereby we can find wholeness in our brokenness, hope in our despair, and victory over death. We can encounter, in a living way, the chastisement that made us whole, and the stripes by which we are healed. In that we participate in the ordering of chaos and the re-creation of human life.

One qualification is needed. Here I am speaking of silence in the context of ritual. I do not suggest in any way that there is no place for the emptying of the mind in the kind of individual silence in which we wait on God, listening to hear him speak. Elijah heard the still, small voice in the utter silence after the hurricane, earthquake, and fire had passed. Contemplative, meditative silence has a vital role to play in the spiritual life of individuals and communities, and space must be made for it in a well-balanced life. But, that is most definitely not what we are about in the silent spaces of ritual. Because we have no training in the intensification of silence in this manner, we find silences in ritual to be similar to breaks in conversation. They are awkward embarrassments, times for clearing of throats and shuffling of feet and sidelong glances to see what our neighbours are doing. It is a feeling akin to not knowing what to do with one's hands when making a speech. Teaching people how to fill and focus a silence must be our goal if ritual is to be as effective as we would have it be.

Sacred Time in Secular Time

"As it was in the beginning, is now, and shall be for ever." Is anything more familiar to us than that phrase? We rattle it off as if it were a single word, tack it on like a suddenly remembered afterthought. Was, is, shall be — three separate times in our reckoning, that is, in secular time. Past, present, and future are the three tenses of daily existence for us. By contrast, to speak of sacred time suggests a contradiction in terms. The sacred by its very nature is beyond time, timeless, before time and after time. This is beyond our comprehension. It is impossible for us to think of before time or after it. But in ritual sacred and secular time become one. "As it was in the beginning, is now, and shall be for ever" is all now in ritual. Ritual provides a way of coping with the terror we feel about time and its passing. Ritual allows us to achieve past-present and future-present in the now.

Past-present is not the mere mental stopping of the clock so as to recollect thoughts about the past. In ritual there is a re-membering, that is, a re-embodiment of the past. We have fought religious wars and burned people at the stake over the meaning of "Do this in remembrance of me." Yet the Greek of the earliest manuscripts is clear in a way our English translations are not. "Do this for my *anamnesis*" should never have been translated "remembrance." To remember in common speech is to recall something mentally, memory work, like multiplication tables or the conjugation of French or Latin verbs. The Greek *anamnesis* is a totally different concept. The word is the Greek version of the Hebrew *zakar*. Both mean to give life to something, to make a contemporary fact or presence of something or someone from the chronological past. In the Hebrew scriptures, quite often it is God who is doing the remembering — of his covenant with his people, for example. The covenant, made once in the past with Abraham, God renews or makes again in a present relationship with his people. It is in this sense that Christ says to his disciples and to us, "When you do this I will be your contemporary, I will be with you." We re-embody, we re-member, his death and resurrection when we make eucharist.

In ritual we recreate time past in time present; more important, we do not leave time present. The sacred is incarnated in the secular, .ot the reverse. We are not taken up into some mystical state of rapture. Ritual is as concrete as the stone of the altar. Future time and present time are equally scriptural and equally a part of ritual; the kingdom is within and among, and at the same moment expected. "Is now and shall be for ever" all at once.

If ever there was a day when the terror of future possibilities weighs on people, it is now. Yet this is not a new experience for the people of God. Apocalyptic visions figure largely in both the Old and New Testament. In history, ritual has been enacted within the shadow of everything from Vandal hordes at the gate to the creeping death of the Plague. We are no different today. Ritual enables us to deal with terror, to make the yet unknown future present in our now. It allows the sacred "shall be forever" to break into and be part of the present. The future-present means that even "if I walk in the valley of the shadow of death," the sacred presence will be with me.

Icons — The Art of Sacred Time

There is, as far as I know, only one art form which consciously sets out to portray sacred time in the secular. It is, unfortunately, not well known and barely understood in the West. It is the icon. Mosaic and painting are the predominant media of the icon. They are often presumed to be the Eastern equivalent of the stained glass and sculpture of Western church art. This is not so.

We begin to grasp the significance of icons when we note that great emphasis is placed on the Incarnation and the Transfiguration. This harkens back to St Paul's words in his letter to the Colossians: "He is the image [Greek, *ikon)*] of the invisible God, his is the primacy over all created things" (Col 1:15). Humanity before the Fall was in *imago dei*, in the image of God. Christ as the Second Adam restores the ikon of God. So in Eastern iconography Christ is often portrayed as the new human, the fully revealed incarnate Son of God. Likewise the saints, when they appear in icons, are portrayed in a transfigured state, fully realized in heaven. They are seen not as they were on earth, but as they will be in the church triumphant.

Orthodoxy makes it quite clear that these iconographic persons are not meant to be a kind of visual aid or picture on exhibition. They are not mementoes of revered ancestors who have gone before. In a sense most difficult for Western minds to comprehend, icons indicate a present reality. In the West we say "Seeing we are surrounded by so great a cloud of witnesses." In the East there is a contemporary presence in the icon which actually surrounds the people. This presence is made known by perspective. If you look closely, you will notice that the lines of perspective (say of a road or a building) which in Western art retreat away from the viewer to a point in the background of the painting, in an icon are reversed and extend to a point behind the viewer. The icon is looking at you, not you at it.

I spoke with a young Orthodox priest about this recently. He told me that when he is on the other side of the iconostasis (the screen separating sanctuary from nave, on which the icons are hung) preparing for the celebration of the liturgy, he hears the elders of the congregation coming forward and conversing with the icons. They speak of their problems, joys, and sorrows. "And," he added, "I swear sometimes I hear answers!" We easily dismiss this as at best fantasy and at worst idolatry. To do either is to admit the poverty of our Western vision. That fact that we can find that sense of the sacred in the secular meaningless or fanciful, illustrates how Cartesian is the world we inhabit.

So much of Western religious art is a flat, lifeless portrayal, rather than the incarnation of what it portrays. Partly this is due to the content of much that passes for religious art in our churches. There is an emphasis on either a soft, sentimental Jesus and the saints, or on Christ dying a violent, agonizing death. Those hold no power to transform, for such images themselves are not transfigured. The mosaics and frescoes of the early church (what representative remains we have) and of the Eastern church even today, portray triumph! Christ reigns in glory or is trans-figured on earth. The saints throng in a great community around him; they too are triumphant, sharing in his victory. In icono-graphy we see captured the *eschatos*, the future triumph. "When God shall have put all enemies under his feet" is now, and in such sacred art we participate in the ultimate triumph over evil.

A major step towards more effective incarnational communica-tion will be taken when we become much more demanding and discriminating about the iconography by which we surround and illuminate our ritual.

Touching and Feeling

I approach this aspect of communication very gingerly. If there is one area of contemporary sensibility in which even angels fear to tread, this is it. For the most part we are terrified of touching. In crowded situations — subways and concert halls, shopping malls and church buildings — we spend an inordinate amount of time saying "Excuse me" because we touched someone. The passing of the Peace is unquestionably one of the most controver-sial aspects of liturgical change, and most difficult to introduce.

I think this illustrates well the power we associate with touching. We know that babies die if they are not cuddled enough. We talk about "not getting enough strokes," and therefore experiencing frustration or even clinical depression. We are conscious of the role of touching in expressing and fulfilling love.

We crave touching and being touched. Thank God there seems to be an increasing recognition and acceptance of this in our society. How often I have stood in air terminals, with all my Anglo-Saxon reserve, and watched in envy as newly arrived people from Italy or Portugal were greeted by their loved ones? The increase in bumper stickers and buttons bearing such queries as "Have you hugged your kids today?" or "How many hugs have you had today?" is at least one encouraging sign that my envy is shared by others. I am also conscious that those immi-grants and their relatives come from a part of the world border-ing the Mediterranean, in which the infant church was formed.

They are familiar with many of the place names which, for me and my ancestors, are only titles of New Testament epistles. They understand far better than I how important is St Paul's admonition, "Greet one another with the kiss of peace" (1 Cor 16:20; 2 Cor 13:12) or St Peter's, "Greet one another with the kiss of love" (1 Pet 5:14).

The New Testament abounds in tactile images and incidents. Peter and John say that God's plans (*mysterion*) "under thy hand and by thy decree [word] were foreordained." The creative power of God is imaged as in his hands; he acts by touching his secular creation. "Stretch out thy hand to heal and cause signs and wonders to be done through the name of thy holy servant Jesus" (Acts 4:30). Instances of Jesus healing and casting out demons "by the finger of God" or by the laying on of his hands or the application of some form of touch to blind eyes, withered limbs, fevered brows, or even seemingly dead bodies are too numerous to cite chapter and verse.

The early church seems to have made much wider use of the laying on of hands and annointing than is done now. Until quite recently, such tactile ministrations were severely restricted in the Western church. This meant that, for the majority of Christians, confirmation became a once in a lifetime experience of sacramental laying on of hands. The minority experienced it a second, third, or fourth time as they were admitted to the holy orders of deacon, priest, or bishop. Annointing virtually disappeared from Protestantism, was barely maintained in the Anglican ethos, and was restricted to a single application at death's door in the church of Rome with, again, the exception being ordination. In some parts of the Anglican communion, annointing and laying on of hands is, praise God, becoming much more common, especially in baptism and the healing ministries.

We have a long way to go to reinstate the validity of the tactile as a legitimate part of communication in the church. We can look again to our artists for leadership. Some modern sculpture — I think immediately of much of Henry Moore's work — cries out to be touched, to be stroked. One of this century's greatest sculptors, Moore is also one of its most prolific and best known. His monumental works may be found in parks, public buildings, and museums throughout the world. Moore's *The Archer* is familiar to millions of people who have gathered in or passed through Nathan Phillips' Square in front of the city hall in Toronto. Perhaps they could not tell you Moore's name, but I can tell you from watching them, that if they stand and look at it for more than a couple of minutes, they will invariably reach out and stroke it! It is interesting to note that in the Moore Gallery at the Ontario Art Gallery, which contains a large collection of the plaster originals from which the final bronze works were cast, there are several prominent signs declaring, *"Please* do not touch the sculptures, they are very fragile."Henry Moore has said, "Really great art enlarges existence into something more than everyday life, giving some kind of importance to it, a monumentality and grandeur." I have no idea whether Moore is a Christian or not, but that is as close as you are likely to get to a nontheological statement about the sacred in the secular. "Art," he has also declared, "has no separation between past and present."[8] (Another example of all-at-once time?) It has been said that Moore's works "inhabit not only three-dimensional space, but the space of memory and dreams."

So, let an artist point the way for us in this. Moore affirms, "Holding things is understanding form. Touching things, making things, helps you understand shapes and forms. You need to use your hands as well as your eyes." To realize fully the potential of ritual, we need to use our hands as well as our eyes and ears.

Surrounding the Space: Light and Music

One of today's most brilliant geniuses of stained glass is Rowan LeCompte, whose breathtaking *Creation* rose window flames in passionate power, lighting not only the west end but the entire interior of the National Cathedral in Washington, D.C. He is responsible also for the awesome magnificence of the nave clerestory windows in that glorious building. Le Compte, speaking of the art which is his love, points to "a more difficult subtlety, the most telling ways of 'painting' with light, articulating light. Intermingled notes of coloured light can so easily be inharmonious, harsh or dull, disorganized, flat or out of control. But they are called to sing. The great windows do sing.

"The parallels to music are many. Like song, stained glass can communicate ideas, can teach. But, like music, its core is aesthetic and emotional. Installed in buildings where it can fulfill — or frustrate — a powerful architectural role in admitting and tempering the light, its primary purposes are more ethereal: It can stimulate the imagination; like music it can lift the heart; it can enchant."[9]

What a delightful word to describe the role of tempered light in stimulating the imagination — *enchant*, to put into the form of liturgical singing. I was privileged to have a conversation with Rowan LeCompte in the Bishop's Garden at the National Cathedral in the cool of a spring evening. This gentle, unassuming master of his craft reminded me of the words of Ervin Bossanyi: "Only works of art done by passionate burning love bear the mark of validity in buildings of dignity." This statement touches on a vital component of all ritual — the surrounding of the ritual space with light and harmony. Effective ritual demands that the air around it, the very atmosphere, be charged with appropriate sight and sound.

Once again there are signs of hope in current liturgical trends. The moving of altars out to chancel steps or nave crossings may have been motivated by a desire for psychological and visual centrality among the people, but it had another result. The central focus of the eucharistic ritual has been moved from the dark cavernous interior of many sanctuaries into a more appropriately lighted area. Inadequate though much stained glass is in our churches, to bathe the altar in tempered light is a vast improvement. Where the natural lighting is inferior — whether in sanctuary, chancel crossing, or nave — it is usually because the stained glass does not enchant; it entombs. Its muddy opaqueness mutes even the sunniest of days into a sepulchral gloom which acts to deaden any lively efforts to breathe life into our quest for the sacred. When this is the case, remedial measures are called for. No, I am not about to suggest the smashing of historic, memorialized glass. Instead, we need to seek professional assistance in augmenting the light. Be careful of consultants, however; what is appropriate for centre stage or TV studio is not necessarily what you need to supply the ambience of your ritual. The light must enchant; it must sing. It must be warm, colourful, lively, shadowless, and inviting, for all of these are part and parcel of the nature of effective ritual.

My nerve falters when I attempt to discuss music. One needs only to travel about parishes even in a small diocese to realize that parish musical traditions are very localized, irrational, long standing, and die very slowly. In spite of all this, surely there are some things we can suggest. First, the hymns, anthems, postludes, and preludes should be very carefully and deliberately chosen to fit the theme of lections and homily. Of course, this implies early planning and study of lections, identifying of themes, and consultation between celebrant (homilist, if not the same person) and music director. Ritual demands, is nourished by, is dependent upon participation. This simple fact can be remembered when choosing musical settings for ritual. Excepting, perhaps, cathedral churches and those who imitate them, settings must be singable, within the range of untrained voices, and used often enough to be familiar. New settings should be rehearsed by the choir and congregation prior to the service for several weeks before use, and then used for a long enough period for people to become comfortable with them.

All of these suggestions are within the capabilities of the smallest congregation, even if it has only a small, or even no, choir. The training, encouragement, and recruitment of choirs is beyond both my competence and the scope of this work. However, we do need to look briefly at the nature and role of the choir as it relates to ritual.

The choir is part of the ritual congregation, not a separate entity. True, theirs is a specialized role of leadership and, if their quality merits it, of special offering. But the choir, its performance and choice of music, must not intrude. It is frustrating when the rhythm, the cadence, of a well thought out liturgy, which to that point has the feel of involved participation, grinds to a halt and falls flat while the choir performs a lengthy piece. The participants suddenly become audience, and the choir ceases to be participant and becomes performer. Now that all choir directors hate me, let me hasten to add how often the sense of involvement in ritual has been for me, and I am sure for millions of others over the centuries, intensified when the air is filled to overflowing with totally appropriate music, at totally appropriate moments. That does not happen, however, without a deep sense of "what is going on here" — careful planning and co-operation, and liberal use of imagination inspired by a vision of the potential for the encounter with the sacred which ritual affords.

12
Monday
to Saturday

In what purports to be a study on communication in the church, we have spent a major amount of time and emphasis on Sunday morning worship in a parish church. There is a very basic reason for this. The fact of life in the contemporary North American mainline church is that the one-and-a-quarter-hour space on Sunday morning is the only time we have with the vast majority of members of the church. We may wish it were not so and hope that it may change, but that is the reality with which we must deal. The percentage of our parish membership that is actively involved in mid-week activities, compared to the number in attendance on Sunday, is minimal. Even then, statistics tell us that on any given Sunday only 30% of those on the membership list of the average parish are in attendance. So, unfortunately, our approach generally is to take advantage of the only time when we have at least some of our parishioners "with one accord in one place." The result does not make for involving, incarnating ritual. There is simply too much else going on, too many other kinds of communication. These other communication functions — such as Christian education, giving notice of upcoming events, soliciting volunteers, fund-raising, and a seemingly endless list of others — are all perfectly valid. They must be done to maintain the secular life of the community. The pity is that, while they are all going on, we are trying to unite heaven and earth in ritual!

The suggestions made thus far, intended to assist the effectiveness of the transfiguring process, would be greatly aided by a clearing of the clutter from Sunday morning. This requires a careful "communication function analysis" of what is going on during that precious time of gathering, and the application of some skills learned from the mass media. It involves identifying target audiences and media options. Without going into elaborate detail, this process may be described as directly opposite to the way in which we normally communicate information in the church. We tend to use the "shot gun" approach. Fill the air with pellets and hope that, with a bit of luck, some poor bird will inadvertantly fly into one. Pew bulletins, notice boards, parish news letters, announcements in church all fall into this category and are our primary tools. They are hopelessly ineffective.

Contrasted with this approach is the "rifle" method. Pick a specific target and aim a single projectile very deliberately. It is here that we encounter the need for very careful identification of the target audience. Who, as specifically as possible, needs to know this? What is the best, most effective way available to reach them? The process of specific communication is a skill which needs to be learned. There are many lay people who, in their daily occupations in advertising or other mass media, use such skills, who would be delighted to be asked to share their professional knowledge. We make little use of them at present. In a book dedicated to exploring incarnational communication rather than the sharing of information about things, no more need be said about this. However, I want to emphasize that this sort of communication is critically important to the life of the church or any other community. Let us simply try to avoid the grave error of thinking it is the only dimension to communication in a living organism.

Now, having acknowledged the critical nature of Sunday morning, we need to ask how ritual, transfiguration, and metaphor apply to what goes on Monday to Saturday in the life of the church. Certainly attendance at worship is not all that happens in a parish, diocese, or nationally in the life of the church. The task of encountering the sacred in our secular challenges us in such activities as educating, the production of audio-visuals, and in opportunities to use television and, increasingly, videotapes. The tools at our disposal are wonderful in their variety and potential. But the prime, overriding principle remains the same. Our efforts must be anchored firmly in the stuff of our ordinariness. For example, one of the responses of Jesus to the perpetual, "Who are you?" was "I am a door." Tell that story with every graphic detail that you can. Then resist the temptation to add, "Now, what Jesus meant was . . ." Instead (if in a teaching and discussion setting) ask for examples of doors in our lives, or (if producing an audio-visual) present some. Doors of opportunity, doors which protect us from what is outside, doors which shut us out, doors to the secret places of our lives, and doors which guard what we treasure. Then, and only then, build the bridge of metaphor. "So when Jesus says he is a door, it is like . . ."

The second necessity is visuality. This applies particularly to the homilist, the preacher, and the story-teller. "Show slides" verbally. Use all the picture language which you possess, and which the story possesses. Help the listeners see the story inside their heads. If you are old enough to remember radio drama (as I am) you will recall how gripping it was. *The Shadow, The Inner Sanctum, The Lone Ranger, Lux Radio Theatre* grasped and held us because their scenes were inside us. That particular kind of writing enabled us to be involved in a manner that no movie or TV production can ever achieve. I sometimes demonstrate this phenomenon to communication workshops by playing, without any advance explanation, an audio tape of the sound of an airplane taking off. As the sound dies away I pause, then ask, "What colour was the airplane?" The grins begin to form. "How many engines did it have?" Heads begin to nod. "Where was it going?" It is quickly evident that each person has created a specific airplane taking off from a specific airport and bound for a specific destination. That is the goal of the verbal communication which incarnates ideas! It is not beyond the reach of our day to day efforts to use such skills in the opportunities available in many teaching or discussion situations.

When we move to the production of resources in which the use of actual pictures is possible —slide or tape presentations, cable TV, videotapes or photo collages — a different dynamic comes into play. Interesting as they are for nostalgia or to share the highlights of a vacation trip with those who stayed at home, slide shows which feature "This is Dad in front of . . ." and "Here is the motel we stayed in at . . ." do little to touch the living core of our imagination. Certainly there is a place in the educational resource library of the church for slide shows or videotapes which tell us about conditions and situations with which we are not familiar and which need our prayers, concerned action, or financial support. They are useful as well for fostering a sense of belonging in the very diverse community which is the world-wide church today.

But we sorely need, as well if not more, visual productions which deliberately leave open the space of metaphor. In such productions, spoken sound track or dialogue is minimal; visuals are graphic, compelling but non-specific. Sound is vital, but it may be the voice of nature, wind, sea, birds, rain, thunder, a child's cry, laughter, or silence. Music can be very effective if carefully chosen to create atmosphere, to lift the inner eye to new vistas, to enchant. Resist the temptation to choose a song because it has appropriate words. Music with words, in this type of visual art, can be extremely damaging. Like spoken scripts, it has the same effect that we observed in story-telling; it says, "Now you see these pictures. What they mean is . . ." Let the pictures mean what they mean to the viewer. Take that risk! You may be running less risk than you do when you use loaded words which can mean so many different things to different people. Frequently pictures are far more universal in their imaginative impact than words, no matter how carefully chosen.

There are many technical tools available to increase the effectiveness of audio-visual material today — dissolves, fades, graphics, multi-track recording. Do not be dismayed or inhibited by limited resources or experience. In most congregations or communities, or near by, there are all the resources you need, both of personnel, and equipment. Seek out the photographers, the TV station personnel, the faculty and students of community colleges of applied arts and technology. My experience is that they are thrilled to be asked, excited to be involved, and overjoyed that the church is anxious to communicate imaginatively. This can be more significant lay involvement in the ministry of the word than all the lesson reading in the world!

We have seen that participation is an integral element of effective ritual. It is no less vital to other forms of communication. Whenever possible, people should be given the opportunity to respond and to individualize their response. This is especially so when the presentation, as described above, is open, imaginative, and non-directive. "Can you express how you reacted to that?" "Did that make any connections with your life and experience?" These are the questions which enable. They do not imply, "This is what it meant. Did you understand?" In expressing response, viewers become participants. Their reaction becomes learning, added to what they glean from the expressions of others. The bonus of this procedure is for the producers. They discover how well their intention was realized, and they gain insight into the *saeculum* of the people with whom they are working. In this time of increasing communication sophistication and capabilities in handling electronic equipment among the laity, particularly young persons, an even greater participation is possible. It is far more effective to provide the space, in an emotional as well as a physical sense, for lay people to produce audio-visual resources to say something of their experience of God in their *saeculum*, than it is to produce something to show them what you think it should be!

None of this is revolutionary. To many in the church, it will be dreadfully old-hat. It is presented with the hope that for some it will be envisioning and enabling. To all, I hope the earlier groundwork in the vocabulary, grammar, and syntax of incarnational communication will be a useful way of approaching much of what we do as word processors. The Word was — is — made flesh and dwells among us, if only we have the eyes to see, the ears to hear, and the fingers to touch and shape the secular stuff of our lives. If the church truly is Christ's body, all our communicating must be as embodied as possible. By this the church really can be the extension of the Incarnation in this day, and tomorrow, and until the day after for ever.

13
Every Journey
Has a Beginning

The following material is not meant to be a definitive guide or a "how-to" text book set of directions. I include here a series of models of things which I have tried, to assist people to move into, or perhaps to discover and realize that they already reside in, a world of metaphor. The emphasis is on experience followed by instruction, attempting to avoid the reverse, which I find is seldom very successful. I believe the sessions follow a reasonable order, but that is not to say one could not do them in a different sequence for some specific purpose. Nor is it to imply that the entire sequence must be followed slavishly, as if it were some authorized curriculum. You might want to try only one or two of the processes, on their own, or as part of some larger goal.

I have tried to indicate the approximate length of time which could be given to each segment. You may find it profitable, however, to take one or more parts of the program and spend a great deal longer at it, to immerse your group or yourself more thoroughly in it.

I   The Things in Life that Really Count

a   Have the group (in plenary) call out the things that "count" for them. List them on newsprint. Things that really *matter* in their lives — those things that have matter, that therefore exist. Discuss (in plenary) how many of these things involve information *about* someone or something — data that could be fed into a computer, versus those which have to do with relationships to someone or something. (15 minutes)

b   In "buzz" groups (2 or 3 where they sit; do not move into groupings) share examples from their own lives of the increasing power of information — computer foul-ups, the disappearance of money as it is replaced by credit cards and automatic bank transfers. This could even get on to a discussion of the role of satellites, spies in the skies. (15 minutes)

c   Leader presents in her/his own way the content of the material in Chapters 1 and 2. (30 minutes)

II   Introduction to Sacred and Secular

a   In small groups (maximum 5 people per group) discuss, "What has the word *secular* meant to you prior to today?" (10 minutes)

b   Small groups continue. A church school teacher once taught his 9 and 10 year old students a prayer to use on entering Church prior to worship: "O Lord, I am in your house. Shut out the world and make me think only of you." Discuss: What does this say to the children (and us) about worship? Is it an appropriate prayer at that point? How would you change it? (20 minutes)

c   Sharing of small group observations in plenary. (10 minutes)

d   Leader presents material found in Chapter 3.
(20 minutes)

III   Signs, Symbols, and Images

Prepare the meeting room by hanging, in random order, around the walls.

— Six examples of signs, such as Stop, Danger High Voltage, Traffic Light, Sign from outside church.

— Six examples of symbols, such as a cross, Canadian flag, swastika, crucifix, star of David.

— Six modern "symbol signs" such as Deer Crossing, male and female washrooms, No Smoking, laundry instructions from clothing labels.

— Six images such as pictures of children and of their parents, a statue of Buddha, picture of a sunset, realistic sculpture.

a   When group is in place, ask them to take 10 minutes to walk about, look at objects, mingle and converse, then be seated. Leader asks a series of questions without at any time referring to objects by name as a sign, symbol, or image. Merely point to or pick up object and ask.

— How does this (sign) differ from this (flag)?
— How does this (crucifix) affect you differently than this (Buddha)?
— What does this (crucifix) say that this (cross) doesn't?
— What are the limitations of these (signs)? (illiteracy, colour-blindness, cultural arbitrary decisions)
— What is the relationship of — a sign to what it sign-ifies?
— a symbol to what it represents?
— an image to reality?
— How is a picture different from a symbol?
(30 minutes)

b Leader presents material from Chapter 9. (15 minutes)

IV Myth

Discuss in small groups
— How do you use the word myth?
— What does it mean to you to hear the early chapters of Genesis described as myth?
— If you could not use the word myth, how would you describe the stories in Genesis, Noah's Ark, Jonah's fishy adventure, and the Book of the Revelation of St John the Divine?
— Can you think of any contemporary myths?
(30 minutes)
Share in plenary. Leader should play it by ear. If material on myth in Chapter 9 has not surfaced, she/he should mention it.

V Moving Towards Metaphor

a Leader tells group a vivid personal incident in which she/he has to use many "it was as if . . ." and "it was like a . . ." phrases. Then leader tells, as picturesquely as possible, the story of Jesus and Nicodemus, or gives several examples of Jesus' kingdom sayings, "The kingdom of heaven is like a . . ."(15 minutes)

b Individual work
Each member of the group works on her/his own for 10–15 minutes. You are writing to a person blind from birth; describe in one paragraph each of these: Lightning

> A Spring (or Fall) day
> A campfire

When completed, each person shares work with one person. (10 minutes)

c In small groups. Could any member(s) of the group share a story of an incident, scene or person they vividly remember. Doesn't have to be "religious" just vividly remembered. (15 minutes)

d In plenary discuss:

> Why do we have difficulty describing these kinds of experience, or this "knowledge" of another person?
>
> How do we "carry over" our experience of a thing, person, or event into the present? (15 minutes)

e Leader picks up on "carrying over" which in Greek is *meta-phora*, and presents material from Chapter 10. (30 minutes)

VI   Epiphany Stories

a Leader tells the group two scriptural "epiphany" stories (see Chapter 5) — burning bush, Damascus road, Emmaus, Isaiah's vision "in the year King Uzziah died," Peter's basket let down from heaven and one contemporary epiphany from either personal experience or that the leader has heard or read. (20 minutes)

b In buzz groups (2 or 3 where they sit) share reaction, response, personal experience. (15 minutes)

Suggestions for "getting into" scriptural epiphanies, or other vivid stories.

— Read the story in the King James version, and in at least three other translations, slowly and carefully.

— Consult a good scripture commentary to become familiar with the context, what led up to and follows the incident, the nuances of the original language, cultural insights.

— Choose one version and read it *aloud* several times. Pay very close attention to the spoken words, to all monologues, dialogues, and conversation.

— Try to concentrate on, imagine, the feelings of the participants.

— Write your own version of the event, using as much descriptive, picture language as possible. One way is to write it as a drama or a screen play for a movie or TV show, including

stage directions, costumes, movements, dialogue. The point is to make it as alive and visual as you can.
— Then, put all your written material aside and tell the story to someone.

It sounds like a lot of work, but it is worth it!

VII   Feeling Sights and Sounds

An audio-visual immersion experience.

The purpose of this session is to help people get in touch with their ability to create mental pictures and to personalize images which are presented to them. Above all, it is to assist them to recognize feelings associated with that mental activity.

a   Play a record or tape of selections (perhaps openings only) from radio serial dramas of the 1940–50 era — *The Shadow, Suspense, Lux Radio Theatre, Inner Sanctum.* Talk briefly about the "world of the inner imagination" where one supplies one's own pictures, which was the stock in trade of such productions. (10 minutes)

b   Project a series of slides (perhaps 20), preferably using two projectors and a dissolve unit if available, no sound track. Slides should be carefully chosen to elicit emotional response. Nature scenes, children, family life, food, dining, perhaps some negative response images such as war scenes or pollution, but not horrific. The recognition of emotional response is our goal, not the statement of any "messages." Each slide should be visible for about 5 seconds. After viewing the slides, ask each participant to describe in writing how they felt, what they could smell or taste, where they "were" while watching and who was with them. (15 minutes)

c   Run an audio tape of about three minutes duration containing sound effects such as an airplane taking off, sounds of nature, gentle wind, seashore, birds, sea gulls, gentle rain, an infant's gurgle and laugh.

  Ask the group to listen with their eyes closed, then write answers to
— Where was the airplane going? What colour was it? What airline?
— Where did it take you? Who was with you?
— Who was the child? What colour hair? Eyes?

(10 minutes)

d Share these "inner landscapes" in triads. Each person takes five minutes. (15 minutes)

e Return to plenary for the sharing of general observations. (15 minutes)

VIII   View a Movie

As a group view a current movie together, either by attending a local theatre (preferred) or by renting a VCR copy. There is no way of knowing what movies will be current or available when you do this, and it is very difficult to describe what kind of movie you should see. Perhaps the only way I can help is to describe how I approached two that I have seen.

For discussion after viewing *Amadeus.*

— Salieri says, "Mozart's music is the voice of God," and that Mozart is "the incarnation of God."
   What do you think these two declarations mean? Are they justified?

— What were the three most vivid images in the movie for you? Can you describe why?

— Each time I have seen this movie in a theatre, the audience has remained seated in complete silence at the end, staring quietly at the lengthy closing credits, then silently filed out without the usual chatter and rush after a movie. Why? How did you feel at the movie's end?

— There is no question that Mozart was a genius. Was he also insane? Was he possessed by God or a demon?

— Mozart's music is glorious. What does the movie's portrayal of his character and the circumstances of his life do to your appreciation of it?

— What was the significance of Salieri burning the crucifix? What does it say about the subsequent events of the movie?

— Think of the last scene of the movie. Relate it to, "O grave, where is thy victory?" Does Mozart's music overcome "the sting of death"?

— We are told that this movie is historically incorrect. Does that matter?

Questions for discussion after watching *2010*.

— HAL, the letters in the name of the computer, are the letters which precede in the alphabet the letters I B M. One of the themes of the movie is the relationship of humans to computers. What does it tell us about information *about* versus relationship *to*?

— The monoliths, regardless of size, are always in the dimensions of 1 X 4 X 9 (the squares of 1,2,3). About them is said they are

> — "very large and seem to have some purpose"
> — "an embassy for an intelligence beyond ours"
> — "a shape of some kind for something that has no shape."

What was your reaction to these strange, symbolic forms?

— There are frequent images and symbols of decay, sleep, death, rebirth, awakening, and rejuvenation in the film. How many of them can you recall? Discuss their significance.

— In the discussion about whether HAL should be told that he and the Discovery must be destroyed, Dr Chandra declares, "Whether we are based on carbon or silicone makes no fundamental difference. We should each be treated with appropriate respect." When machines possess intelligence and can think, what is the appropriate respect that we should give them?

— "HAL was told to lie by people who find it easy to lie. HAL doesn't know how. So he couldn't function. He became paranoid." "I don't know if HAL is homicidal, suicidal, neurotic or just plain broken." What was your emotional, feeling-level reaction to HAL?

— The final message of the film is "We are only tenants of this world. We have been given a new lease . . . and a warning from the Landlord." Compare that with the Genesis says about humanity's role in relation to the created order.

The idea of this movie exercise is to assist people to begin to look for the signs, symbols, images, myths, and rituals which are all around us, and especially in what we usually call "the media." In addition to movies this includes popular music, TV, popular fiction, advertising, magazines.

Obviously not all the questions can be addressed. The discussion should run for about an hour in groups of not more than six. Perhaps different groups could be assigned two or three questions each, or each group could be asked to make its own choice and try to address three questions. There should be plenary sharing after the group time, but not a "report back" from each group separately.

It would seem easier to spend an evening together watching regular commercial TV programming. You may wish to do that. The difficulty is that TV is so much a part of the fabric of our *saeculum* that it is extremely difficult for most people to "step back" far enough to be able to observe it, without some advance preparation and training.

For an approach to TV which provides that training and preparation and assists people to assess more deeply its symbols, images, rituals, and their impact on us, I recommend the *Television Awareness Training* program. Information about it can be obtained from Resources for Ministry, 600 Jarvis Street, Toronto, Ontario M4Y 2S6, or the national headquarters of churches in the USA.

IX   Implications and Ingredients

Chapter 11 — Speaking Publicly and Hearing Privately
          — Response and Participation
          — Touching and Feeling
          — Surrounding the Space: Light and Music

Not everyone will agree with the positions taken in these sections of the chapter. Certainly most participants in workshops on this material will find the thoughts expressed in them to be quite foreign to their experience of worship in the vast majority of parishes. Not all leaders will agree with this material sufficiently to want to use it at all. However, if one wishes to, I would suggest that each section be presented separately by the leader to the whole group (about 10 minutes). Then small groups of four or five share their experience around these two questions:

— How does my experience of public worship compare with,

agree or disagree with, what I have just heard?

— How would I change my parish's worship (if I could, and if I would) in the light of this?

This small group discussion should not run more than 15 minutes; then the leader presents (again, about 10 minutes) the next section, repeats the small group discussion on the same questions, and so on. The session for these four topics would consume about two hours, including a break at the half-way point.

X   Common, Communication, Community, Communion

To explore the inter-relatedness of these four concepts based on the root idea of sharing something which creates unity or union.

a Tell three stories (use method of preparation previously described).

    i Genesis 3:especially vv 8 – 15 and 23, 24.

       God and his friends can no longer walk together, enjoying a chat in the cool of the evening, sharing and being at one with the environment. The images change to hiding, shame, broken communication, weeds, pain, banishment. Sin has destroyed community, communication, and communion.

   ii Genesis 11:1–9

       Pride again destroys not only community but the ability to communicate, to know each other, to understand.

  iii Acts 2:1–11

       The holy spirit creates a new community, and its first manifestation is the ability to communicate, to hear the performative communication of the Lord, to know and to understand.

       (15–20 minutes)

b Questions for discussion in small groups. Time the discussions. After 15 minutes ask groups to move on to next question.

— In the light of these three stories, develop a definition of communication (not more than two sentences).

— What barriers to communication, as you have defined it, can you identify in the community in which you live, and in the parish in which you worship?

— Does holy communion create community, or does it grow out

of community?
— What would you need to do to enable the Sunday eucharist in your parish to express community better?

XI   One Place to Begin in Your Parish

The normal, main service on Sunday morning in St Average's parish church is a mixed bag in which real community and effective ritual are difficult to achieve. There is a quite legitimate reason for this. We're too busy doing other very important things. I mean that with no sarcasm. What we are doing is very important. The questions are, "What is it that we are doing?"and "Could we be doing it some other way at some other time, perhaps better?"

One way to get at those questions is a Communications and Community Functional Analysis of Sunday morning. Sounds impressive. It might be worth doing just so we could say that's what we're doing! It is best done on the site physically, but it can be worked at by a group in a workshop setting, if they share a lengthy intimate experience of the parish. This is not nearly as effective as being there, but can sometimes be a prelude to the real thing.

The analysis is an examination of everything in the physical environment and in the activities in it on a Sunday morning. Everything in the physical environment, from the parking lot in — signs outside, the building, the grounds, furniture inside, room arrangements, washrooms — everything! As well, every single human activity which can be observed comes under the analysis.

It is done quite simply. Each participant has a number of separate pages, each with a heading, and divided into two vertical columns. Over one column is "Hinderances"and over the other "Contributions." The page headings are

1   Information Giving/Notice Boarding
2   Community Building
3   Christian Education/Instruction in the Faith
4   'PepRallying'/Encouragement/Enthusiasm
5   Fund Raising
6   Entertainment
7   Social Action

You may want to do this from memory in a workshop session as a training exercise, before doing it ''for real'' in the parish. In an actual parish situation you should have a group of at least a dozen people involved on several consecutive Sundays.

In either case, the individual lists are compiled on to a master list, eliminating duplications, which becomes the basis for discussion of the following questions, as an aid to planning future action.

— Examining each function, ask, ''Is there a way we can do this better, perhaps at some time other than Sunday morning?
— What functions are better done elsewhere so that worship and ritual may have pre-eminence?
— How can we do better those functions which are necessary and appropriate on Sunday morning?
— If reality demands that some (or all) of these functions be done on Sunday morning, how can we create other worship ritual spaces in the parish?

Notes

T.S. Eliot, *Collected Poems* (London: Faber & Faber, 1958), pp.157,159–60.

Archibald MacLeish, *The Human Season: Selected Poems 1962–1972* (Boston: Houghton Mifflin, 1972), P.135.

1 Rene Descartes, *Discourse on Method and Meditations on First Philosophy,* Trans. Donald A. Cress (Cambridge: Hackett Publishing, 1980) P.57.

2 George Steiner, *Language and Silence: Essays on Language, Literature and the Inhuman* (New York: Atheneum, 1970).

3 James Joyce, *A Portrait of the Artist as a Young Man* (New York: Viking Press, 1959), p.174.

4 Herbert O'Driscoll, *A Doorway In Time: Memoir of a Celtic Spiritual Journey* (San Francisco: Harper & Row, 1985), pp.77–78.

5 Thomas Driver, *Patterns of Grace: Human Experience as Word of God* (San Francisco: Harper & Row, 1977), p.xxiii.

6 William J Bausch, *Storytelling, Imagination and Faith* (Connecticut: XXIII Publications, 1984), P.19.

7 Basil Spence, *Pheonix at Coventry: The Building of a Cathedral* (London: Geoffrey Bless, 1962).

8 Henry Moore quoted in article in *Art News,* May 1983.

9 Rowan Le Compte, "History and Techniques," in *Jewels of Light: The Stained Glass and Mosaics of Washington Cathedral,* Ed. Nancy S. Montgomery and Marcia P. Johnson (Washington, D.C.: Protestant Episcopal Cathedral Foundation, 1984).